START & RUN AN
ADULT BOUTIQUE

Start & Run an Adult Boutique

Karen Bedinger, MA

Self-Counsel Press
(a division of)
International Self-Counsel Press Ltd.
USA   Canada

Self-Counsel Press acknowledges the financial support of the Government of Canada through the Book Publishing Industry Development Program (BPIDP) for our publishing activities.

Printed in Canada.

First edition: 2008

Library and Archives Canada Cataloguing in Publication

Bedinger, Karen
   Start & run an adult boutique / Karen Bedinger.
   Accompanied by a CD-ROM.
   ISBN 978-1-55180-834-5

1. Specialty stores—Management. 2. Selling—Sex toys. 3. Sex-oriented businesses.
4. New business enterprises. I. Title. II. Title: Start and run an adult boutique.
HF5439.S46B43 2008   381'.4568   C2008-904893-8

Self-Counsel Press
(a division of)
International Self-Counsel Press Ltd.

1704 North State Street
Bellingham, WA 98225
USA

1481 Charlotte Road
North Vancouver, BC V7J 1H1
Canada

CONTENTS

Part II — Maintaining Your Business

Part III — Merchandise   125

12 Adult Toys   127

13 Clothing and Shoes 139

14 Accessories, Novelty Items, and Adult Movies 147

Acknowledgments

I dedicate this book to my husband, Daniel Bedinger.

Dan helped immensely in the preparation of this book. It all began when he first helped me set up my own adult boutique, which is where much of the details of this book stem from. He tirelessly applied his vast array of skills, used almost all of his free time, and put a lot of hard labor into helping me open and operate my store. In the writing of this book, again he helped me. I would like to thank him specifically for his encouragement, his guidance, the countless times he read this book, his suggestions for revisions and ideas for text, and his wonderful understanding during the times it took me away from our free time together.

My sister, Dr. Tina Cartagena, spent a lot of time and effort reading my first version of the book. From her edits, she helped me to write a better book and focus on writing a more technical versus personal book. Her time, effort, and encouragement are all deeply appreciated.

My mother, Doris Scheiwe, and mother-in-law, Gail Bedinger, provided me with encouragement and the time to be able to write this book. They acted as teachers, playmates, babysitters, and loving grandmas (omis) to my adorable baby son. Thanks to the grandpas for letting the grandmas travel long distances to do these things! We are very lucky and grateful to have such loving grandparents.

I would also like to thank my father-in-law, Michael Bedinger, for being a big help in the initial start-up phase of my store, as a web programmer, painter, mover, and carpenter.

Notice to Readers

The author, the publisher, and the vendor of this book make no representations or warranties regarding the outcome or the use to which the information in this book is put and are not assuming any liability for any claims, losses, or damages arising out of the use of this book. The reader should not rely on the author or publisher of this book for any professional advice.

FOREWORD

For as long as I can remember, I have always wanted to own my own business; it sounded fun and rewarding. Besides, working for someone else never made me happy. However, as great as it sounded to be a business owner, I knew it would not be easy. Thus, before I completely dedicated myself to owning a business, I weighed the pros and cons.

The pros seemed great; after all, that was why I was interested in owning my own business. First of all, I liked the idea of having the freedom to decide for myself how, when, and where I needed to accomplish my work. Working for someone and having him or her tell me how to do things all the time was irritating and distracted me from my goals. If I owned my own business, I would know how the company was performing and be able to have an effect on its future.

The ability to control a company's performance, outside of economic or other unpredictable factors, means being able to manipulate every aspect of a company from its finances to its level of customer satisfaction. Most of the time, an employee is not even privy to the company's inner administrative workings, much less able to control any or all of the factors that affect performance! As the CEO of my own private company, I would be able to control almost everything about the business. This also meant that I would decide who got laid off and who got raises. No more working my butt off so a CEO could make his or her million-dollar bonus, while I scraped by making the standard raise just above the inflation rate. This time, I would reap the monetary benefits of working smart and hard.

I also wanted to own a business that would benefit my community. Sometimes, it seems nearly impossible to get good products and services at the same time. Providing products and services that could make peoples' lives a little bit easier or happier made me happy in return. Knowing that I could be the one to deliver these things to my future customers gave me the motivational drive to create the best boutique in town!

Out of all the wonderful and idealistic reasons for wanting to own my own business, most of all, I did not want to wake up every day and drag myself into work feeling like I was the main character in the movie *Office Space*. Instead of feeling like I was doing the same thing over and over again, I wanted to wake up energized and excited to get to work, because once there I could get things done the way I wanted to. And if anything got redundant, I could do it a different way.

Despite the many pros, the cons of owning a business were still going to exist whether I wanted to acknowledge them or not. Therefore, I decided the best way to prepare for the cons was to be informed and try to avoid them. The biggest con was the risk of losing a lot of money, time, and possibly my sanity!

The potential to lose money instead of make money can be very stressful. So can the possibility of failing due to unforeseen consequences or as a result of your own missteps. If you use any of your own money to start the business, you could lose it if the venture does not prosper financially. The best way to make sure you do not suffer losses is to do the proper research, work diligently, and be smart about how you set up the business.

My husband and my father-in-law helped start my business; although it was difficult and stressful, it was something that we accomplished together. By viewing the venture as a project we could do together and have fun with, we ended up spending more time with each other instead of less time. They also gave me feedback on my business ideas, provided new ideas, and helped immensely with physical and administrative labor.

Starting and maintaining a profitable business is hard work, so I sought ways to make it easier and more enjoyable. The very first step in ensuring I wouldn't get easily burnt out by managing the store, was choosing a type of business that I was interested in for reasons other than just making money. This connected my work with a personal hobby, so that when I worked on maintaining my store it was fun. I was interested in the latest lingerie fashions, curious about the newest adult products, excited to find the hottest trends for Halloween costumes, and happy to be working with people.

One of the last hurdles I needed to overcome to maintain my business's success was to keep my family, friends, and myself happy. In the beginning I spent almost all of my time either running, talking about, or thinking about my store, instead of separating it from my everyday life. I was so obsessed with how well my business was performing that I began to forget to make time for anything else. Eventually I realized that my business's success could not simply be measured in profitability; rather, it also had to be measured by the way in which it affected my family, my friends, and the quality of my life.

It is easy to allow your business to overwhelm your life. Even if you are not relying on it to bring in income, you may feel like it is a part of you because you sacrificed a lot for it and put a lot of hard work into it. Therefore, most people want their business to be as perfect as can be all the time. They spend all of their time working hard to improve the business or worrying about it.

Remembering that your business is not a complete reflection of who you are and that you have to allot time for the other parts of your life, can greatly help you to keep the business in perspective. This is especially true when you are using both your store and your home as places to work. Physically separating where you work is as important as mentally separating your work from your life. When you dedicate time to yourself or your loved ones, you need to be mentally as well as physically unattached from your work. This can be done by leaving your thoughts, paperwork, and other business-related work at the store.

Making time for your regular hobbies is also important. At first you may not have time for this. However, if after you have opened your business for a couple of months you are still not devoting any time to your hobbies, it can be a warning sign that you are spending too much time working on your business.

I thought I knew all of the hardships and delights of owning a business before I owned one. After I opened my own, I grew to appreciate that if a person has never owned a business, it can be very difficult for them to fully understand how demanding and rewarding it can be. By writing this book, I hope to provide you with ways to

mitigate the hardships of owning an adult boutique business, so that you can focus instead on the rich rewards.

The following is the story of how and why I decided to open an adult boutique.

1. The Journey to an Adult Boutique: Materialization of an Idea

"How about opening a type of classy, couple-friendly adult boutique?" My husband, Dan, asked me as we were brainstorming ideas for opening a business.

"What?" I exclaimed.

"Yeah, why not?" Dan asked.

"Uhh … " was all I could muster.

"Remember when we thought about how great it would be if there was a nice adult shop in our town?" Dan responded.

"Of course I remember that, but I never actually thought about doing it myself!" I proclaimed. "I have such a straight-laced appearance … and I'm a bit conservative … I'm not sure I could interest people in my store," I sputtered as I tried to come up with excuses as to why I couldn't do it.

"Well, it was just a suggestion. Why not give it some thought?" my husband replied.

"Sure," I retorted cynically.

I had been thinking about opening my own business for a couple of years. Ideas about the type of business I wanted to open had been bouncing around in my head and included everything from a bakery or floral shop to a private business consulting firm, but I had not yet considered an adult store, so I was a bit taken aback by his suggestion. However, Dan and I had only driven two hours into our eight-hour road trip to Orange County, and since there were no distractions along the boring I-5 freeway, it was hard not to think about his suggestion.

I started reminiscing about the first time we visited an adult store that didn't make me feel like I had to wear a bag over my head when I left it. It was a store in San Jose that we had been hearing about for a couple of years in an advertisement on the local radio station. The ad explained that the store was a great place to purchase something for your sweetheart and a fun place to go shopping as a couple. It was a few days before Valentine's Day and we thought it sounded like fun to go there for our date with Cupid.

I did have some misgivings about going to an adult store. We had been in a few adult shops before, and I usually left them feeling like I had to go home, turn on all the lights, and take a shower to wash away the dirty smell and feel. However, we were always looking for new adventures to experience together and this did sound like one of them — so he didn't need to try too hard to convince me to go. The next day we got in the car and drove south on the freeway for more than an hour to get to the store and see for ourselves what it was like.

The building was split into two separate stores that stood side by side. The one on the left seemed a bit more welcoming than the one on the right, even though it was not much more attractive. It had handpainted billboard signs that looked like they had been put up overnight, that advertised gifts and toys for adults. The building looked like

it needed a new coat of paint; the dark purple exterior was peeling and fading and we could hardly see inside the store. I wondered if we had driven for so long in the cramped car for nothing. The other store looked like a typical adult video store with a bright neon sign and blacked out windows. Neither made me want to rush in and browse.

I was still leery to go inside either store, so we chose the shop on the left that looked a little more inviting. To my surprise, we were greeted by friendly and well-dressed staff. I looked around for the grunting, disheveled and smelly sales guy, but to my delight, I never saw one. In fact, the shop was entirely different from any adult store I had previously visited.

There were also none of the other things I was expecting from an adult store: no funky smells, no dirt on the floor, no messy stacks of merchandise, no dark corners, and no loud noises or music playing from an adult movie. Instead, I was impressed by how the store smelled like vanilla, how it was clean and airy, how beautifully the merchandise was displayed, and how busy it was with both male and female customers. Either the store was already very popular or the radio advertisement was really paying off! That was when I knew I had walked into a different type of adult store, because it felt as though I had just walked into any other type of nice retail establishment. If it were not for the merchandise, I wouldn't have known it was an adult boutique.

The merchandise included a vast array of adult toys with a small selection of lingerie. There was everything from erotic lotion to "back" massagers, and what seemed to us like contraptions meant to either tickle or torture someone. Although the helpful staff explained what some of the items were, I never thought that I would ever come to know what they were all used for!

Since we had such a great experience in the first store, I felt even more adventurous and decided that I was now willing to go into the video store next door. Was I ever disappointed! Because the exterior of the building was similar to the other store, I had expected it to be similar inside. However, when we walked inside the store, I was shocked at how different it was. First of all, I didn't see any staff right away and when I did, sure enough, it was that unapproachable guy I had assumed would be in the first store we went into! I felt like I had just walked into an adult store stereotype. There was trash on the floor, the lighting was too bright in some places and too dark in others, there was no air conditioning or ventilation. There were no prices on anything, which meant that customers had to brave asking the employee (who was watching a pornographic movie) in order to ask him how much something cost. I quietly murmured to Dan, "Yuck! Get me out of here!" We turned around and walked out.

As optimists, Dan and I tend to look on the bright side of our experiences and that day was no exception. We had a lot of fun and achieved what we had set out to do. It made me feel like we were on one of our first dates again, even though we had been together for so many years. We had managed to spend time alone together doing something exciting and fun. The experience led me to think about all the things that could help sustain a fresh, healthy, intimate, adult relationship.

As we drove home we talked about how neat it would be if there were more adult stores like the first one we had gone into, so that we didn't have to drive more than an hour to get to one. We lived in a highly developed metropolitan area, yet there were still few adult stores around. We thought these stores would be less likely to concern communities if they didn't appear so unattractive, and looked more like other retail stores or even had exteriors that were more beautiful than other stores. As we talked about what we liked and disliked about the store, we began to create in our minds the ideal adult store for women as well as men.

In our opinion, the ideal store would be like this: The store would be located on a main street of a town or city. It would have a beautiful exterior and the windows would display tasteful products like pretty lingerie on fancy mannequins, and part of the inside of the store would be visible from the outside so that people would not be afraid that if they entered they would never return to the outside world again! Since window browsers could see part of the inside of the store, we thought that upscale lingerie and other pretty accessories should be displayed in the front of the store, and more racy toys and items should be kept in the back of the store. It would be sparkling clean, comfortable, and well lit; prices on products would be well displayed; and the staff would be professional and helpful.

It seemed a good idea to make a one-stop-shop for all the intimate adult merchandise a person could want. A store with a broad selection of lingerie that included everything from the traditional to the more upscale and racy, along with adult toys, novelties, party supplies, and DVDs. It would be a fun and practical place to go shopping. After all, why did the video stores have to be separate from the shops with other merchandise and why did they have to be so displeasing to the eye? So far, there were many upscale lingerie stores (including two mega national chain stores) nearby, but they did not carry adult toys or DVDs. Lingerie stores were only for adults, so it seemed like a natural continuation of the merchandise to include these other items as well. By partitioning the store so that lingerie was separate from the adult items, one could still attract customers that were only interested in the more conservative or conventional items.

We continued to daydream about the ideal adult store for the rest of the day. However, it still hadn't occurred to me that I could one day open an adult boutique.

Now, while Dan was driving us to Orange County, the idea seemed to set in my head. I had to admit that it did sound like fun and that all my other ideas did not seem as enjoyable or practical.

Who was I kidding — I was never an early bird, so owning a bakery was probably not a good idea. I also liked the idea of owning a floral shop, but fresh flowers spoil easily, and for that matter, so do baked goods. The retail shelf life of lingerie, on the other hand, is as long as the style is current. When it is out-of-date, a store owner can place it on a clearance rack and still make money on it. Although I wanted to continue to work in the field I received all my schooling in

and had worked in for so many years, I also wanted to experience something different, and starting a business-development company just didn't seem very exciting. The idea of an adult boutique seemed like much more fun.

I wondered if there would be enough business for my shop to make a profit. Thinking about it practically, I knew that there was enough business for almost any kind of product to sell; it's all about presentation and advertising. After all, the cookie was invented long before Mrs. Fields began selling them. However, at the time I was not sure how many people purchased adult products. What came to mind then was my experience working at Victoria's Secret. Dozens of people had asked me if I knew of any other stores that sold lingerie that was different from what they sold there. I had not known of any besides the other main retail chain stores, but people were looking for even more choices. I figured that if these businesses did well enough to be huge, national, profitable chain stores and people were still asking for more choices, there was room in the marketplace for additional competition and merchandise. Combining the sale of lingerie with adult products would only increase revenue.

After giving the idea of opening up an adult shop a couple of hours, I proclaimed to Dan, "I'm going to open an adult boutique and it's going to be awesome!"

This time it was his turn to be a little shocked. It only took him a couple of minutes to recover before he jovially asked, "Does this mean you'll be modeling a lot of lingerie for me?"

2. The Mainstream Prevalence of Adult Products

The more I thought about the idea of owning my own adult store, the more I liked it. Retail is not the easiest business to get into, as there is so much competition these days, but my idea for a store had a huge advantage over other stores because of the scarcity of nice adult stores and the fact that there were no really nice adult chain stores yet.

The fact that adult products and DVDs are becoming much more accepted in major retail shops and in mainstream media makes it easier to sell these products. On top if it all, the marketplace is only slowly catching up to cater to women and couples.

Adult products are sold almost everywhere. A person can purchase lingerie in major department stores, at Victoria's Secret, and at Frederick's of Hollywood. A person can purchase adult toys in the mall at Spencer's, and "massagers" at The Sharper Image and department stores. Lubricants, massage oils, and other intimate adult items can be purchased at the local drug store, grocery store, or major retail chains. Adult movies can be purchased in many local mini-marts. Advertising for adult products is also becoming more prevalent on radio and television, and in newspapers and magazines. For example, KY® Brand advertises their lubricant and massage lotion on network TV and in mainstream print magazines.

Adult movies and stars are also becoming more accepted in mainstream life. The most famous adult pornography stars such as John Holmes, Ron Jeremy, and Jenna Jameson are as well-known as many top Hollywood actors. There have been dozens of pornography stars that have been in mainstream movies, on television, in the news, in documentaries, and in music videos.

Racy lingerie products such as crotchless panties and shelf bras are no longer deemed sleazy. They can now be purchased from upscale lingerie retailers, and are no longer confined to small, out-of-the-way shops hidden in the mall. When almost everything sold in an adult store is also available at the mall, it is usually safe to assume the purchasing power in North America has embraced these products.

3. Finding the Perfect Model of an Adult Boutique

Right before I announced to Dan that I was going to open an adult boutique, I began thinking about possible names for the store in my head. This was when I realized that starting an adult boutique was what I was going to do. When I decide on something, there is usually no going back — it's full speed ahead from there!

I began scribbling my business plan on anything I could write on: little scraps in the glove compartment, some loose paper in my purse, the backside of a map. Since I had written business plans before, I did not have much trouble thinking of a rough outline: possible company names; a mission statement; and a description of my business, marketing plan, costs, profit analysis, business structure, financing, and future goals. Of course, I was going to have to research, figure out, and verify a lot of the information in my business plan and write it out in more detail. But at that moment, it was helpful to have an outline of what my company was going to be like. By the time we arrived in Orange County, I had written the first draft of my business plan.

We were staying with my sister and brother-in-law that weekend. When I told them that we had decided to open an adult boutique, I was not all that sure they believed that we were definitely going to do it. After all, I still had a few nagging doubts. However, being as helpful and encouraging as they always are, the day after we arrived they took us to three different adult stores in Orange County that were aimed at couples so we could gather more ideas of what other adult boutiques were like.

It was important to me to visit more adult stores so I could figure out if I would enjoy owning and managing an adult boutique. I tried to imagine being the owner of each adult store we went into and what it would be like to deal with customers and employees, as well as order merchandise, price the products, and perform all the other daily and administrative work involved. From what I could tell, the customers in each of the stores that closely resembled the type of store I wanted to own — a store more oriented towards women and couples — seemed very nice and normal. The owners of the stores were often working in them when I was there. Most were very open about how they started their business and what it was like for them to own an adult store, and were usually enthusiastic about providing me with advice on how to open and operate an adult boutique.

We paid attention to what we liked and disliked about each store so we had an idea of what to model our store after. Even though I like to work fast, I have always wanted to know as much as I can about a topic I am working on before I start my projects. So on our way back from our vacation we took a different route home and stopped at a few more shops in Los Angeles.

During the first couple of weeks after we returned home, while I began to work in earnest on my business plan (along with the initial setup of the business), we visited more stores in Sacramento, San Francisco, Santa Cruz, Berkeley, and Lake Tahoe. We also went to other upscale clothing and product stores to compare what made the adult stores feel so different in ambiance. It was not necessarily the merchandise that made the difference, it was the clothes racks they used, the paint on the walls, the carpet on the floor, the type and quality of the music or deadly silence in the background, and all sorts of other details that completely changed the landscape of the way the stores looked and felt.

In no time I had a list of everything I did not want my store to be like, and what I did want it to be like. Sure enough, I came up with an outline of a store that was very similar to the ideal imaginary adult store that Dan and I had thought of originally when we visited those stores in San Jose. First and foremost, I wanted the store to cater to both male and female customers. I wanted my store to make women feel comfortable when shopping, but I also realized that there was a point where male customers would not feel comfortable in the same store if it was geared too much toward women. Balancing the store so that both sexes would feel comfortable in it would not be difficult as long as I kept that in mind. My store name and logo would have to portray this women- and couple-friendly atmosphere so that people would recognize it as a place for them to shop.

Aesthetically, I wanted the store to always look beautiful on the outside as well as the inside. Of course that meant it should always be clean, well-lit, have professional employees, and have an air of sophistication. I took note that the neighborhood the store was located in was very important. As a woman, I also did not want to be afraid of the neighborhood where I was shopping, and I did not want to go somewhere that was run-down. The color of the store, inside and out, was important as it could make a customer think twice about entering. Blacked-out windows and dark paint were definitely out, as they would make it look seedy.

The professionalism of the staff would be just as important as the merchandise and the setting, because they would help create the ambiance of the boutique. Because I wanted the store to be more upscale than any of the others I had seen, I wanted everything from the hangers and hooks to the dressing rooms to be beautiful. Dressing rooms with just a curtain hanging in front of them, that did not close all the way, would not fly in my store — they would make a person feel like he or she was the star in a peep show!

Important information I gathered while visiting other stores included a list of brand names that I wanted my store to carry and notes on how other stores were pricing their merchandise. If I thought a particular lingerie outfit or adult toy was appealing, I would jot down the brand name and research it on the Internet to get more information

about the manufacturer and other products they might carry. I kept track of other items I saw that I wanted to sell in my store, such as shoes, handbags, hosiery, wigs, jewelry, bachelorette supplies, birthday supplies, and adult greeting cards. There is no magic formula for deciding what items to carry in a store, so I went with my instincts.

After creating a model of the type of store I wanted to own, I had direction and my work seemed more straightforward.

4. Honesty, Perseverance, and Hard Work

When I began to hear stories of other adult boutiques being shut down by city officials, or their leases not being renewed or being manipulated by landlords due to the adult content of the stores, I started to worry whether my idea was sensible. A few people in town had also hypothesized that the city would not allow an adult boutique as there currently were no others. I did not want to spend a lot of time and money on something that was never going to materialize so I decided to research the stories and issues I had heard about.

My research uncovered that most of the stories I had heard were not true; if a store was shut down, it was because it had illegal activities going on or there were zoning issues. Of the stories that were completely false, I had found out that the stores were actually still in business despite small protests by their communities. The stories of adult businesses being shut down because of illegal activities did not worry me because I was not going to let anything illegal happen in my store! The only real concern I had was about city zoning laws.

Not one to create a lot of controversy, I decided the best step forward would be to inform myself about and become involved in the local business community as much as possible before I opened the store. After I purchased a city zoning map, I asked the city zoning commissioner if he could advise me of any additional restrictions that could be placed on the type of store I was going to open. He asked me to provide him with a short business description for the city's review. I decided to give him not only the business description but also a description of the type of people who were going to run the store to show him my intention to run a professional business. While he had the department review the case, I did background research.

I called the police department and they referred me to the city attorney. She said that the type of store I was going to open would not violate any city laws. I also researched the city code laws on adult stores just to be certain. My store was not actually going to be a traditional adult store: I was not going to have any live entertainment or viewing facilities, and would not offer services. In order to avoid the principal purpose of my store being for adult usage, I made sure that more than 50 percent of my merchandise was in retail clothing such as lingerie, shoes, and hosiery (instead of adult toys or novelties).

When I was looking into opening my store, it was difficult for any small-business owner to find a good location in my town because a lot of the business realtors only wanted major national chain stores or restaurants in their locations. As an additional hurdle, none of the realtors wanted a store that sold any kind of adult material.

Persistence paid off though, and I finally found a location for my business. Even though it would have been easier to avoid telling the realtors that I was going to sell adult items, I did not want to have any problems renewing or keeping my lease. I never could verify any stories of landlords kicking their tenants out due to merchandise restrictions, but I did not want to have to worry about it either. Keeping myself and my store in good standing with my landlord helped me to negotiate a good lease, bring in customers, and avoid grief.

Although it seemed that there weren't any restrictions on my business, I kept up my vigilance to make sure nothing would go wrong between my store and the city. I attended city hall meetings and joined a few key local business clubs in the community. Before long, it felt as though most of the business owners in the community knew me and that I was going to open an adult boutique. I encouraged them to ask me questions about the store and provided them with information about it. They grew to understand that my business was going to liven up the somewhat-depressed downtown area, be beautiful, and bring in business for their stores as well. I began to feel that I was part of the business community before I even opened my doors. Thus, when the time came to actually open, not only did I already have the support of the city officials and business community, but I had also made a few customers!

When I first opened, I did have a few protesters. The police would come in to inspect my store, but of course, they could find no problems with it. Most of the time they would come back when they were off duty and purchase items! Because I remained active in the community and kept my store very clean and neat, mosy people accepted and supported my business.

After consulting with fellow adult boutique owners, I realized that most of the problems they were having were the same as those any other business owner might have. They would get burnt out working too many hours during the day and end up doing things like not opening during the hours they said they were going to, being rude to customers, not performing their administrative duties (such as ordering and stocking merchandise), or not checking up on their employees to make sure they were operating the store correctly. Even the best-kept boutiques can start to deteriorate if the owners are not working at maintaining status.

I am sure there are other reasons why some adult boutiques have closed, but progress cannot be made when one is too focused on the reasons why a business could fail. Focusing on how to make a business a success and working hard at it is the best way to make sure that it will be successful.

INTRODUCTION

It is really not that difficult to start and run your own adult boutique, and if you take the time to read this book, it will be even easier. This book outlines the steps necessary to start your own adult store and keep it running smoothly and profitably.

I will share with you the information I have learned from obtaining my Master's in Business, helping other people start their own businesses, and owning my own adult boutique. My partner and I started an adult boutique called Naughty Or Nice Boutique in the historic part of downtown Vacaville, California, and more than two years later business was still fantastic. In the store's first full year of business, it had more than $200,000 in sales, and in the second year of business, $250,000 in sales. The store's sales continued to grow every day while I owned it. After 25 years I was able to sell the store at a profit. It can take hard work and long hours to get started, but owning your own business comes with many rewards.

Choosing to start an adult boutique over another kind of store has many benefits. The financial benefit comes from the fact that there are not yet any major national retail chains selling sex toys — which means that a new adult boutique has few stores to compete with. Also, there will always be customers looking for your products — almost every adult wants to have fun with adult toys sometime in his or her life, so no matter how conservative the town is, the customers will be there. This is especially true in recent years as more people acknowledge and embrace their sexuality.

Opening an adult boutique provides a social benefit by creating a comfortable atmosphere for both men and women to shop for intimate items to enhance their sexual well-being. By providing a valuable service and having a large portion of the adult population as your potential customer base, you are bound to create a profit.

Although more and more adult stores are opening every year across the country, there are still not very many in comparison to other types of retail stores. That is why now is the perfect time to open an adult boutique and create an established business before there are adult stores in every town. With this book you will learn exactly how to start and run your adult boutique, and with some hard but rewarding work, it will be a success!

1
THINGS TO CONSIDER BEFORE YOU BEGIN

The decision to start and run your own business is a big one. You must consider many things before you spend the money on setting up a store. Owning an adult boutique is not everyone's cup of tea even if it does sound like a lot of fun. This chapter discusses the first things you will need to consider to find out if starting and running an adult boutique is the right choice for you.

1. Do You Have the Motivation?

Do you have the motivational drive to accomplish your goals, as difficult as they may be? In the heat of the moment you may say "yes" quickly. However, it is very common for small-business owners to discontinue their business because they are burnt out from all the work, or to have their business flounder because they do not put as much time and effort into it as they need to. If you are a smart and hard worker, you will find a way to make your business prosper, but without motivation, your business may never become a reality, much less profitable.

Working long hours, especially when the work becomes difficult, takes a lot of dedication. It also takes a lot of determination to perform your duties well. Before deciding to own your own business, it is imperative to ask yourself what kind of worker you are, realistically, in your everyday life — because you are most likely not going to change your work habits once you decide to own your own business. If you are not a self-motivator and rarely ever take the initiative to get things done, you will be in trouble. No one is going to be there to make sure that you do all the things you need to do, never mind ensure that you do them correctly! Unless you are someone who lives by a mantra of getting things done and getting them done right, your dream of owning a profitable business may become the nightmare of owning an unsuccessful business, or it may never become more than just a dream.

Praise from an authority figure must not be your motivator because there will be no boss to give you any praise. A lot of your everyday duties, besides making the store look nice, will be behind the scenes of your store; for example, negotiating with your vendors for better prices or fixing a plumbing problem. Since your customers do not see this type of work being done, they will not be complimenting you for a job well done. Knowing that you have done a good job must be satisfaction in itself, which may be difficult to remember when you are working long hours.

Operating and overseeing your own business is like having two jobs, except that you are not sure when you are going to get paid for them, and you will not receive recognition for a lot of the work you do. You will have to wait patiently for any monetary rewards, because often a new business takes time to become profitable — sometimes six months to one year, or longer. However, if you work diligently you may start to see profit, and you may receive praise from your customers, which can be extremely rewarding.

2. Can You Manage Criticism?

Another question to ask yourself is whether or not you will be able to handle criticism and possible harassment from people with a negative opinion of adult boutiques. Even the oldest and most modest adult boutiques have received negative feedback from some people. Many times this negative feedback is minuscule compared to the positive feedback. However, it can be difficult to cope with and some people handle it better than others. You will most likely be able to mitigate the amount of complaints you receive by carefully choosing the type of image your store portrays as well as its location.

When I first opened my adult boutique, I had several people complaining to the police department or writing in to the local newspaper that my store was too risqué to be located in Vacaville. When I discussed their complaints with them, they were usually the same people that complained about stores such as Victoria's Secret, Frederick's of Hollywood, or Spencer's. This made me realize that their complaints were not actually against my store, but were complaints against stores that sold items they did not want other people to buy. These complainers did not want to allow others the ability to choose for themselves what they wanted to buy because of their own beliefs. Fortunately, when the complainers spoke to people other than me, the only thing they accomplished was to give me free advertising by letting other people know about my store. Besides the word-of-mouth exposure, some of these complainers even became customers once they realized that they could not stop other people from shopping at my store!

3. Will You Do the Research?

Several factors helped me keep my head above water and produce profits sooner than other stores. I kept my current job as I researched the market, wrote my business plan, got all the paperwork in order, talked with business advisers, and found my location. I had already received my Masters in Business, but if I had not, I would have taken some classes in business at a community college or some other place while I was working.

There are also sources such as the Small Business Council of America (SBCA), Canada Business, local business offices, the Chamber of Commerce, and other business resources that you could get assistance from. A good library, bookstore, or Internet site will also have some excellent information about whatever part of the business that you do not fully understand. Receiving industry newsletters will also help you to learn about your specific industry.

Getting involved with local business associations will keep you informed with local business politics in your community. In doing so, you will also be able to have your say in any changes to regulations or laws that may occur in your area, and you can try to proactively shape the local business politics into something better for your store. Associations such as the Chamber of Commerce are also great resources for information on where to get help with a business concern or for general information you may

need to start your business. Becoming involved with business associations will also help you to network with other entrepreneurs at functions.

The next step I took before opening my business was advertising and participating in community events. This allowed my future customers to anticipate my store opening.

One of the biggest decisions I made was when to open the store, as I had to figure out what would be most beneficial. I decided that the best time would be a month before the Christmas holiday season, which is when people generally spend more money. I planned to open the store on November 30, which was centered around a tree lighting festival in the downtown area. The planning of this opening was crucial because thousands of people were in the area that evening, which provided the business with many customers and free advertising.

Try to open your business during a season when customers are more likely to spend money. The biggest season by far for an adult boutique that sells retail clothing is the month of October (for Halloween). December is the next biggest season because of Christmas, followed by Valentine's Day in February. June and July are also big seasons because of weddings and anniversaries.

Researching the best time to open your business will help give you a projected date for opening it, which will allow you to set a time line for when you will need to get all of your preparation work done. Without having a time line to accomplish your goals, it is easy to procrastinate and either open the doors a lot later than projected or never at all.

4. Are You Prepared Financially?

Being prepared financially usually makes work easier and allows a business owner to do the job better. This is especially true when preparing to start your business, as the process can be extremely stressful both mentally and financially. The following are some tips on how to alleviate these stresses.

First of all, if you are not cash-rich, keep your current job until you absolutely cannot work both jobs anymore. By doing this, you can start envisioning your business and getting a taste of what you are getting yourself into before you bite off more than you can chew. Keeping your current job will also help pay your bills, and you will hopefully save some money to help you through the months when your store is open but you are not yet making a profit. Budgeting for your personal bills when you open the store is just as important as budgeting for the bills that you will need to pay for the business.

It is difficult to know how much extra money you will need to have saved to start your business and keep it running, as you will not know exactly how much you'll be earning in profit. A general rule of thumb is to have enough cash to pay your business and personal bills for at least three to six months. It took several months for my business to start making a marginal profit, but it is common for a non-chain retail business to take up to six months to a year to break into the profit zone, depending on the type of store it is and how the start-up is executed. Even if you are buying an existing business with an established clientele, you cannot be 100 percent sure of how much you will be making, so it is always wise to have a little more savings than you think you will need to pull through any difficult times.

The old mantra that it takes money to make money still remains true in the retail industry. Therefore, it is better to have more money than you need to start your business, rather than not enough money. When money starts flowing out of your checkbook like water, it becomes natural for some people to want to halt this flow. For example, some business owners may decide to stop advertising or to not order as much inventory, which may lead to lower sales and ultimately harm profits. Therefore, if you have already dedicated yourself and are taking the risk of owning a business, you will need to have the stamina to make sure that you are constantly making the correct choices for your business, even when you begin to feel nervous about spending.

A business is like any other living entity; it needs constant care and attention in order to make sure that it is continuously doing well.

Part I
Starting Your Business and Settling In

2

RESEARCH THE MARKET AND FIND A SUITABLE LOCATION

As you will see in this chapter, researching the market to find the best location for your store is a must. The type of adult boutique you own could depend on its location. First you need to understand what types of adult stores there are, and then you can start looking for available spaces. After you have found some possible locations and have done your market research, it will be easier for you to make a decision about what type of store you want to open and where you want it to be.

You may also decide that instead of starting a new business you want to purchase an established one. Section **3.** discusses starting a new business versus buying an established one.

1. The Different Types of Adult Boutiques

An adult boutique can be as sleazy or as classy as you make it. Historically, adult boutiques were created to attract male customers, so they were not as welcoming to women. Store characteristics such as reputation, image, location, lighting, merchandising, and the type of employees were less of an issue for customers because they were mostly men. However, things are beginning to change as more women feel empowered to take care of their own sexual needs and go into adult boutiques themselves. This has created a wider variety of adult boutiques. Of course, some men also appreciate the adult boutique atmosphere that the women- and couple-friendly stores now offer.

There are three main types of adult boutiques:

- Adult video stores
- Adult bookstores or adult superstores
- Women- and couple-friendly (WCF) adult stores

These different types of adult stores compete with as well as complement each other.

1.1 Adult video stores

The adult video store typically rents and/or sells mainly adult movies, adult magazines, and a small assortment of adult toys. You will usually find these types of stores in larger cities. If you do find them in smaller cities and towns, they will usually be on the outskirts.

Most of the time they have covered-up or blacked-out windows so that people passing by are not privy to the contents of the store. For this reason they are not usually the most attractive stores from the outside. They tend to be in plain square buildings with few frills. These types of stores usually have large, sometimes neon signs advertising what kind of store they are so that potential customers will still notice them.

Except for the subject matter of the movies, the inside set-up of an adult video store tends to look similar to any other video store. Some are more decorated than others with movie or movie star posters, and some spend more money on such

things as the carpet, paint, check-out stand, and DVD racks. However, on average, adult video stores spend less money on their infrastructure than other video stores, so decor is usually limited to the posters they get from vendors advertising their latest movies and rows of pornographic videos displayed on plain, metal video racks. Sometimes they have bins with cheap or on-sale movies in them; these start to look messy if unkempt. Similar to other video stores, the bulk of the movies are organized on the racks according to their genres.

The main reason adult video stores are created is to sell and rent adult movies. Therefore, they carry more adult videos and have a greater selection than most adult bookstores and women- and couple-friendly (WCF) stores. While WCF stores carry most categories of movies that are geared toward their respective clients (discussed further in the WCF adult stores section coming up), adult video stores carry all types of adult movies. An exception is that some may not carry as many instructional videos or films created specifically for couples as WCF adult stores.

Near the cash register, most adult video stores will have lubricant and condoms for sale as add-ons to a customer's purchase. Sometimes they will even have a small selection of adult toys. Very rarely do they have more than about 20 different types of toys displayed for purchase. The toys they sell are usually male masturbation toys and dolls, and general no-frills dildos and vibrators.

There is usually only one person working at the cash register in an adult video store, so customer assistance is very limited.

If there are more employees working in the store they are usually busy stocking movies or doing other work, and it is obvious they were not hired to do customer service. Sometimes the employees will be able to recommend movies, but they are almost always only able to recommend male-targeted titles. Their employees are almost always male, and they are never dressed in anything more formal than tennis shoes, jeans, and t-shirts.

The bulk of customers in adult video stores reflect the above-mentioned employees: they are usually casually dressed men. At about 5:30 p.m. there are men dressed in work clothes or suits because they have just gotten off work. Besides this clothing distinction, there is no other general group distinction that could be made of them. Customers are made up of all ages, classes, ethnicities, and professions.

Women make up a small percentage of the customers in adult video stores, and are usually irregular and infrequent shoppers. Because there is still quite a large amount of men that prefer to shop for pornographic movies without many women present, these stores are ideal places for these men to shop.

Although there are a lot of places for people to find adult movies online, people still like to shop at video stores for several reasons. Some people will always want to shop in brick-and-mortar stores. Other people might not want these videos on their computer. The retail shops with Internet sites are taking advantage of both of these markets.

1.2 Adult bookstores or adult superstores

Adult bookstores and adult superstores are usually the same type of store. The term adult superstore seems to be replacing adult bookstore. These stores sell and/or rent adult movies and sell a greater variety and abundance of sex toys than adult video stores. Additionally, they sell adult novelties and will usually have a small selection of lingerie. Sometimes, these stores will have viewing booths (frequently referred to as video arcades) or peep-booths.

Adult video booths are single person booths in which customers can privately watch or preview the movie they have chosen; it is like a one-person mini-movie theater. The video booths have a TV behind Plexiglas, a button to change the channel, and a bill-taking slot to put money in. The interior is usually very sparse, either steel diamond plate, Plexiglas, or smooth plastic — all very easy to clean. Many cities have ordinances saying these booths cannot have doors that go all the way to the floor or that completely hide the inside, but these rules are frequently not followed.

Sometimes these booths are meant for viewing live nude performances. When this is the case, there is usually a clear plastic covered viewing hole in the peep booth, through which the customer can see the area on the other side of the booth, where there is a nude performer. These booths are usually adjacent to the room in which the merchandise is for sale, or the areas are separated by a wall.

Stores that have adult video booths are considered adult entertainment businesses; therefore, they usually have additional restrictions placed on them by the city or county. They may require a specific adult business entertainment permit, and additional restrictions may involve management criteria of the establishment, cleanliness, locality, noise level, floor plan layout, and other design aspects of the building and parking lot areas.

The exteriors of adult bookstores or adult superstores are almost identical to those of the adult video stores mentioned in the previous section. However, they tend to have more large signs around them that advertise that they sell adult toys and novelties, and thar they have booths (if applicable). These signs tend to be either plain, plastic, professional signs, or appear as if they were hand- written or painted on large boards. Of course, there are always exceptions to these observations.

In large cities, adult bookstores are commonly found in downtown red-light districts or adult districts with multiple adult stores and strip clubs. However, if they are located in smaller cities and towns, without large downtowns, they are often located off the beaten path. These out-of-the-way places are usually zoned for some type of commercial business, and are a specified required distance (appropriated by the city) away from schools, parks, residences, and churches.

The interiors of adult bookstores vary from unattractive stores to cute retail shops, as more of them are starting to improve their appearance to compete with an increasing number of women- and couple-friendly (WFC) stores. Originally, owners of adult bookstores did not pay much attention or spend a lot of money making the inside of the store look nice. Since adult toys were hard to come by in the first place, it seemed to be that shop owners simply displayed their merchandise as easily and inexpensively as they could.

On average, the merchandise in traditional adult bookstores has not been well organized and the racks used for display have been simple. Stores were not well lit, their paint was usually just a plain color, there was no decor, sometimes the floors were not clean, and if the shop had x-rated video booths, noises from porno movies could sometimes be heard throughout the rest of the store. Of course, in an adult bookstore that had video booths, some of these characteristics were in violation of the restrictions mentioned previously.

The floor space for merchandise in these stores is typically dedicated to approximately 65 percent adult videos, 15 percent adult toys, 10 percent lingerie, 5 percent adult novelties, and 5 percent adult magazines. Of course, this number greatly varies depending on each store.

Much like adult video stores, adult bookstores usually carry almost all categories of pornography. They too may not have as many instructional and female-produced videos as WCF stores. The attractiveness of the packaging is usually not considered when these stores buy adult toys, and so their selection of toys may not be as pleasing to the eye as their sister products at WCF stores.

Lingerie at an adult bookstore is usually poorly displayed and is often sold in individual boxes or plastic bags. If the lingerie is displayed, it tends to be hung on simple racks and still be on the plastic or thin metal hangers that the manufacturer used to ship them.

The customer service at an adult bookstore is usually better than at an adult video store but not as good as at a WCF store. Good customer service is often hit or miss. Female employees are not very common, and the male employees usually know something about the toys and movies designed for women, but are not experts on the subject.

Customers at adult bookstores are commonly the same people that go to adult video stores, with the addition of more women and couples. Since there are not yet as many WCF stores as adult bookstores, these may be the only place for women and couples to shop for adult products in certain areas.

1.3 Women- and couple-friendly (WCF) adult stores

Women- and couple-friendly (WCF) adult stores greatly vary in the types of items they sell, where they are located, and the types of employees they have. The main difference between these stores and others is that they are trying to attract more women and couples as customers.

As a result of trying to attract more women and couples, WCF stores have a number of commonalities. They are always clean inside and out, the name of the store is usually catchy, and they sometimes have a logo. The merchandise inside the store is well organized, the store is well lit, the employees provide friendly and helpful customer service, the adult magazines or adult movies are rarely in hard-core genres, and there is never any adult entertainment (such as video booths). In general, these stores make more of an effort to appear and act like other mainstream retail stores.

Typically, the exteriors of WCF stores are more attractive than those of other adult stores. They usually have a pretty and relatively fresh coat of paint, are in good repair and are clean, and most of the time the shop's signage is professional and artistic.

Depending on what the store sells, they may or may not have covered up windows. Covered up windows are often a result of municipal laws that say something to the effect of "Adult businesses must not have their insides visible to passersby." Even if they need to cover their windows, WCF stores still make an effort to appear classy and stylish from the outside. For example, they might use white, opaque glass instead of black boards to cover the windows and they could have pretty drawings on the glass or other decorations on the outside of the store to offset the covered windows. If the store sells lingerie, it will most likely have dressed-up window displays with mannequins in lingerie or costumes, and/or pretty products.

As a result of WCF adult stores' efforts to appear more mainstream (and the fact that they do not have any live adult entertainment), they are more often than not located in the downtown area of cities and towns of all sizes. They can also be found in multi-use commercial areas and areas in which there are mainstream retail shops.

In an effort to attract a greater margin of women and couples as customers, the interiors of WCF stores almost always look clean and well organized, and keep the presence of graphic nude pictures to a minimum (if they're present at all). This ensures the stores appear inviting to the more conservative shoppers. There are two distinctions among the types of interiors that WCF stores have: the more simplistic, and the upscale.

The most common interior of a simplistic WCF adult store has clothing and products displayed on modest retail fixtures, pleasing paint on the walls, and merchandise displayed in its respective categories. Since most of these stores are small, they can become cluttered, as merchants will try to fit a lot of merchandise in them; otherwise, they are much the same as other retail shops. For most WCF shops, there would be no noticeable difference except for the merchandise.

The other type of WCF adult store interior is that of an upscale store, which is becoming more common. These stores spend more money and effort to make the shop look classy and elegant. The effect is much the same as other upscale retail clothing stores. The interior is painted in beautiful colors, there might be decorative moulding or beautiful artwork on the walls, the merchandise fixtures and furniture are more expensive, the merchandise is displayed better, and other small but distinct details are attended to, such as music and attractive lighting.

The interior colors of a WCF adult store are normally light and pleasing, such as a soft, mint green, lavender, or almond shade. These colors are not too bold and yet they provide a feeling of warmth. Decorative items on the walls also add to the aesthetics and warmth of the store. However, when stores start to use more than structural decorative items (such as moulding and wall textures), decor can take attention away from the store's merchandise.

Retail fixtures, furniture, and equipment come in different styles and prices. When these items look nice, they add to a store's overall aesthetics. For example, if a store carries lingerie, displaying it on wooden or heavier, metal hangers versus cheap plastic ones will make the lingerie look more appealing. Or, high-end glass showcases or armoires can be used to display more expensive products to highlight their worth. A buyer identifies half of an item's worth in the way that it is presented to him or her. Therefore, the customer expects an expensive item to be displayed in a beautiful setting and appear valuable if he or she is going to pay a hefty sum for it.

A customer's sense of smell and sound does not turn off once the person enters the store. In fact, in an adult store many customers (especially women) are super vigilant about their surroundings because they may be a little nervous to be there in the first place. Because the owner of a WCF store is trying to attract more women and couples and keep them browsing longer, he or she should ensure that the smells and sounds in the store are pleasant. Fresh air ventilation is important in keeping sweaty and musty smells away. As an added bonus you can fill the space with nice smells, such as vanilla or cinnamon; these smells do not need to be overwhelming, like in some candle or perfume shops.

Often WCF adult stores will have background music playing. This helps customers relax and distracts people that get nervous when they're the only customer in the store. WCF stores tend to play classical, jazz, big band, or modern pop music. The genre of music sometimes depends on the mood the store's owner is trying to set or the theme of the store.

It is sometimes difficult to think of all the things that can make a customer a little anxious about being in an adult store. For example, one day a woman in her mid-30s came into my store with an anxious look on her face. She explained to me that she was very worried because her hand had touched something wet and gooey while opening the door. She said she wanted to scrub her hands. From the look on her face and the use of the word "scrub," I saw that she was imagining the worst. I could not fathom why our doorknob was wet so I went to go feel it for myself. The doorknob was slightly damp and not dripping wet with goo as she had imagined. As customers in an adult shop are not only super cautious about their surroundings but also every now and then a bit paranoid, it was no big surprise to me that her description was way off! I realized that I had just come in the door with a soda can that had been sweating a little from being cold, and my hand had probably gotten the knob a little damp.

There will be times when a customer's imagination will run away from him or her, but finding ways to keep the shop clean, beautiful, and free of things that may fuel a customer's anxiety will help reduce his or her stress of shopping in your adult boutique.

There is a lot of variation in the products that WCF adult stores carry. Typically, they will carry adult toys, novelties, books, instructional and noninstructional adult DVDs, and bath and body products. Many will also carry lingerie, costumes, shoes, jewelry, and wigs.

As an added service to their customers (and often an additional source of revenue), some WCF adult stores will also offer classes and host events. Some of the most popular of these include: pole dancing classes, fashion shows, instructional classes, and adult toy parties.

Pole dancing classes are becoming increasingly more common among all types of women. They provide a workout while teaching students how to dance provocatively using a stripper pole. These classes and other types of events are usually conducted in the store after retail shopping hours are over. They also encourage sales of at-home stripper poles and kits.

Fashion shows are a great way of advertising and getting repeat and new customers into the store. These customers are able to view how the lingerie and other clothes look on models. There is usually food and drink at these events. People are able to relax in a comfortable, laid-back atmosphere and enjoy their visual shopping experience.

Instructional classes are also good avenues to bring customers into the store and provide them with a valuable service. These classes cover topics related to sexual health and well-being, such as safe sex, various types of sexuality (such as bisexuality), intimacy or experimentation (such as bondage or anal), relationships, and specified uses of products (such as corset wearing). These classes tend to be hosted by experts in their respective fields. For example, some classes will be hosted by sex therapists, marriage counselors, authors, or other people working in the field.

Adult toy parties, commonly called passion or pleasure parties, are events in which one or more sales associates inform a group of customers about sex toys and sensual body products (e.g., edible body dust and chocolate body paint) in hopes of making sales. These events are much like a show and tell. The salesperson will show the group of people a product then tell them how it is used and, if appropriate, they might do a demonstration. Finally they will pass the item around so that each person can experience the product first hand. These parties are hosted in the store for customers after hours, or more often in a home for a private group of people. Sometimes, when a customer asks to have one at their house, it will be hosted during a birthday or bachelorette party. Other times the party is thrown simply as a fun women's or couples' event. Many people charge an up-front or higher fee if the party is going to be co-ed. Pleasure parties that are "women-only" tend to have better sales than co-ed or couples' parties.

The main staples that a customer can almost always find for sale in a WCF adult store are adult toys, novelties, safe-sex products such as condoms and dental dams, and sensual bath and body products. As with all of the categories of products that WCF stores sell, there might be a higher or lower ratio of these items in comparison to other items for sale in each particular store.

Carrying adult toys in a WCF adult store is a must. However, the scope of the selection in WCF stores varies greatly. The more conservative shops choose to carry only the more mainstream products, such as vibrators and dildos. Other, less conservative WCF stores will carry a broader selection of adult toys.

The biggest difference between the products sold in WCF stores versus other adult stores is usually the packaging. Whether a WCF store chooses to carry a greater or lesser selection of adult toys, they will usually still choose to carry the products with more subdued packaging. The same type of adult toys can often be purchased wholesale with different styles of packaging. Usually, WCF stores choose to sell toys in packaging that doesn't have crass graphic nudity (or nudity at all) on it. Other differences in packaging include color variations, sleekness, text, and size. Some of the main manufacturers that WCF stores purchase inventory from include Topco Soles®, Adam & Eve®, Vivid, Jill Kelly, Doc Johnson™, California Exotic Novelties®, and Hustler®.

There are two main subcategories usually found within an adult novelty section: gag gifts and adult-related party supplies. It is more common to find gag gifts in these stores than party supplies, because customers purchase these items more frequently (mainly due to the fact that they can be purchased as everyday gifts as well as special event gifts). Party supplies are sold generally for bachelor, bachelorette, and birthday parties. These items tend to take up a lot of space in the store, because stores need to carry a minimum inventory level of many different items in order to please customers. For example, if a customer comes into the store to purchase party decorations, many times he or she will want to purchase the whole setup for the party (such as plates, silverware, cups, balloons, ribbons, and signs). The customer will also want to purchase enough supplies to cover each guest at the party. When a store uses valuable merchandise space for these items, it takes away space for other, more profitable merchandise, such as adult toys and DVDs.

WCF adult stores generally carry bath and body products. These items include: sensual massage oil, lubrication, bubble bath, and candles. These items help to offset the hard-core image of an adult shop and make the store appear more mainstream. Furthermore, customers expect to see bath and body products in a WCF store and might go into the shop specifically to purchase them. Shy or first-time customers might only feel comfortable enough to purchase these products. Bath and body products are great sellers among new, shy, and experienced customers alike.

Adult books can also be found in WCF adult stores. The more popular books tend to be those with subject matter that is not available for purchase on a DVD, or fun, interactive game books, where a person has to open a perforated page or scratch for hidden messages.

Instructional adult DVDs are very popular in both the more- and less-conservative stores. If a WCF store carries DVDs, they usually only sell them and do not rent them. Even if they don't sell a lot of DVDs, they will usually still carry instructional DVDs on conventional topics such as massage, sexual positions, and foreplay. More hard-core topics such as double penetration and bondage are usually found in stores that carry a larger assortment of instructional DVDs.

Fewer WCF adult stores carry non-instructional adult DVDs. They most often carry x-rated videos in more conventional genres, including movies about couples, gay or bisexual men and women, masturbation, voyeurism, and oral sex. Genres that are more hard core, such as "cum shots," sadism and masochism ("S&M"), and bondage are not carried as widely in WCF stores. These types of movies are less common because they are considered to be less appealing to most women, and make the store seem more intimidating to a wider audience. This is also why WCF stores tend to mainly carry a majority of movies that have plots and that are produced by more high-end, respected companies, such as Wicked Pictures®, Adam & Eve®, Andrew Blake, Digital Playground®, Vivid Entertainment Group, Penthouse Classics, and Playboy.

Noninstructional adult videos will not usually be predominately displayed and customers might have to look through the merchandise to find them. If the store is small or the owner does not want to split the store into sections, then it is wise to keep the merchandise with graphic sexual pictures on its packaging hidden away from the more conservative shoppers.

Not all, but many WCF adult stores sell clothing items. The most frequently carried items are lingerie, costumes, hosiery, and boas. Stores typically carry clothing for women, and might have a small selection of lingerie and costumes for men. If a WCF store carries a good selection of high-quality clothing and displays the clothing nicely, the store will draw in more shoppers. This is because some shy customers that want to buy adult products feel more comfortable in a store that looks like a lingerie shop. Additionally, many shoppers coming into the store to purchase lingerie or clothing end up purchasing other romantic bedroom accessories, such as tickle feathers, foreplay games, and satin masks. There aren't many retailers that sell beautiful and sexy lingerie and there are even less retailers that sell other more exotic items. Therefore, a store that carries both has a great advantage for bringing in more customers.

Shoes that are often referred to as "stripper shoes" are sold in a fair amount of WCF adult stores. These shoes are usually high heels, sandals, and boots that have heels on them that are taller than three inches. Carrying shoes has both its pros and cons. A good selection of shoes is not always easy to find, so when a store does have a good variety, they will most likely have repeat customers. Word-of-mouth usually gets around among shoe fans if a store has a good selection, and as a result the shop may attract a substantial amount of new customers. Shoes also make fabulous add-on sales to purchases of clothing and costumes.

The downside of selling shoes is that it might be hard to keep all sizes in stock for a smaller store, because shoes take up a lot of floor space. The size of the boxes and the quantity of them (as a result of the many different sizes a store must carry to have a good selection and size range), makes it difficult for a store to avoid dedicating a lot of space to the storage of shoes. Therefore, some manufacturers only sell whole sizes. Carrying only whole sizes is a good alternative for smaller stores that still want to carry shoes, because this means there are fewer to keep in stock. Once in a while, a customer may not purchase the shoes they wanted because the shop does not carry their half size; however, most of the time if a customer thinks that the particular shoe is not made in half sizes, they will settle for the nearest whole size that fits them best. Carrying fewer styles also allows a store to carry each whole shoe size because there are not as many shoes to keep track of ordering and stocking.

Sometimes, when a WCF adult store carries a lot of clothing items in the store, they will section off the adult content (i.e., the adult toys, novelties, and movies) from the clothing items. Doing this lets them allow people younger than the age of 18 to shop for clothing items without seeing any adult content. In many areas, the adult content is not allowed to be viewed by minors. When businesses are legally permitted to allow minors in their stores, it is because the adult toys and novelties on display have no nudity or graphic sexual content on the packaging, and the products are not shaped anatomically.

Carrying clothing and shoes can help to tone down the hard-core image of a store. In some areas, when more than 50 percent of the products in the store are non-adult merchandise, the store is legally not an adult store. Therefore, these stores are sometimes easier to find a location for because they do not have many of the restrictions that come from being called an "adult store" (and they tend to create less controversy among the most actively judgmental, conservative community members).

There are many other products that WCF adult stores might carry. Other products that are less commonly carried include adult magazines, club wear, jewelry, purses, wigs, and party masks.

Adult magazines are not as popular in WCF adult stores because they tend to be more hard core, with raunchy names. When customers are not purchasing magazines frequently, profit can be lost because older magazines will not sell well and must be quickly replaced.

There are usually more female than male employees working in WCF adult stores. More women are interested in working in these stores, so it is easier to hire them. Also, it is advantageous to hire women because female shoppers are typically more comfortable talking with female employees. Female employees also make the stores appear less like other adult stores, where a customer would usually only see male employees.

The employees at WCF stores are also more professional than those at other adult stores. This is because of their readiness to provide friendly customer service, their in-depth product knowledge, their more stylish attire, and their professional mannerisms. For example, employees in a WCF store will generally never watch x-rated movies in the store, stare blatantly at customers, crack rude jokes, or make offensive comments or suggestions.

WCF adult stores have the broadest range of customers compared to all other types of adult stores. There are normally just as many female shoppers as there are male shoppers, and in the stores that carry more clothing, there tend to be even more female than male shoppers. This is also true if a store does not carry a very big selection (or none at all) of male adult toys or DVDs. Even if there are not a lot of products for men at these stores, they will often still attract men who are shopping for other couple-related products or for gifts for their intimate partners.

Most customers in WCF adult stores are between the ages of 18 and 60 years old. Customers in these stores are often young adults, as the stores are relatively new and younger people tend to be more open-minded about going into new stores and trying new products. Also, older men are usually more interested in the adult movies, and WCF stores typically do not carry a great selection of them.

Shy and conservative men and women are also more commonly found shopping in WCF adult stores than in other adult stores. These stores are less hard core than the others so customers find them less "deviant." There are also other items in the store that they can look at while taking a glance at the adult products. Furthermore, these shy customers can say that they purchased a non-adult item if they are worried about being seen coming out of an adult shop by someone they know.

Just like other retail stores, they are busier at peak shopping times during the day and during holidays. Additionally, the type of customers that shop in the store are a reflection of the type of people vacationing or living in the area. Therefore, there are slight variations in the type of customers each store has, regardless of the type of products they sell.

2. Location and Market Research

The old real estate mantra: "location, location, location" is still around and is just as important to your business as it ever was. A location that has a lot of street and pedestrian traffic in a neighborhood in which people typically have excess spending money might be difficult to get for an adult-type business, but it is worth trying as hard as you can to get one. Foot traffic can be a significant part of your revenue, and customers like going to places in which they can get a lot of shopping done at one time (hence strip malls and indoor malls). However, if your store is somewhere most people do not want to be seen going into, then you probably want a location where there is not as much foot traffic.

2.1 Visit your potential competition

Deciding what type of store to open may depend on what types of adult boutiques currently operate in the area. If there are adult video stores and bookstores in the area, a women- and couple- friendly (WCF) store would most likely do good business, because there could be people shopping for products in these other stores who would prefer to go into a store that was more geared toward women and couples. Often, women will shop in adult video stores and bookstores even though they feel uncomfortable in them, just because they are the only stores around. However, the majority of women would prefer an adult boutique in which they feel comfortable shopping.

You may wish to open a more traditional adult video store or bookstore if there are a lot of couple-oriented stores, so that you will be offering additional products to the existing clientele in the area. There may even be potential customers not shopping at these other stores because they would prefer to shop among the larger selection of DVDs that video stores carry, and might only be able to find the movie they are wishing to buy or rent in that type of store. Also, some people would prefer the adult store they shop at to have video arcades. Video arcades can potentially make up a large portion of your sales.

The WCF adult store and the adult video store or bookstore can work well together in the same town or area because they can refer clients to each other. In the county in which I set up my store, the nearest adult store had an arcade, rented movies, and was not often frequented by women. Because my store did not have an arcade, sold movies but didn't rent them, and didn't carry a large selection of hard-core movie genres, I referred customers looking for these things to the other store. In return, the other store referred people to my store when a customer was looking for items that my store sold but they did not.

You will need to do some research in order to make an educated guess on how well your business will do financially. First, find out if the adult boutiques are a declining or an emerging market in the area in which you are interested in locating your store. From this information, you should also be able to find out how much local competition you are going to have. If there is no local competition, you will need to find out if there is a market for your products.

If there are a lot of adult stores in the area, you will have to figure out whether you will have a broad competitive advantage over any of these other stores in order to win some of their customers and create new customers in the market. Then you will want to deduce how well these local businesses are doing financially. To assess the level of business the nearby stores are doing, go into them and make conversation with the managers. The managers will most likely tell you how their stores are performing. Also, visit a number of these stores on various days and at different hours to see how busy they are.

You can also compare your notes with a more generalized idea of what the industry trend is by researching the profit margins of public companies that sell lingerie and/or adult products. For example, you can obtain public companies' annual reports online or by requesting them in the mail. When you receive the document, review it thoroughly. It will provide you with a general idea of how well the company is performing. If you want to be more thorough with your analysis of a company, you could run some financial ratios and equations on the financial statements provided in the annual report. This can be somewhat difficult to do, and I suggest purchasing a book on reading financial statements to assist you if necessary.

Keep in mind that the scale of publicly-traded companies can be quite different from that of an independent start-up. However, getting a general idea of your industry helps to predict how these stores might fare

in the future. Also, as an added bonus, reviewing large companies' annual statements will often provide an attentive reader with many good ideas for how to run a retail company.

A good way to figure out which direction the market for adult stores in your area is headed, is to find out how many adult businesses are currently in the area, and compare that number to how many there were five years ago. It is easy to find these numbers by looking at informational listings in old and new phone books, researching on the Internet, and asking around town. Even if you think you already know this information, there may be more competitors in your area that you are not aware of. You may never have noticed these other businesses before because they were in a bad location, they never advertised effectively, or for some other reason. The results of this research should show you whether adult boutiques are becoming more or less popular.

After locating all of the adult boutiques in the area, pay these stores several visits. By visiting these stores, you will learn —

- whether the stores are easily accessible by car,
- the type of neighborhoods in which they are located,
- what images they use for their store fronts, and
- how many customers visit their stores.

It will then be easier to accurately judge how long the drive is between your proposed location and your competitors', what type of adult stores they portray themselves to be, and how much business they get on an average day (if you have been there several times on different days, as well as during different times of the day).

Do not shortcut your research by limiting your viewing to the outside of the store. Make sure you go into the store. Going inside will enable you to find out —

- what types of items they sell,
- the variety of items they sell,
- what brands they sell,
- what their prices are,
- what their customer service is like,
- how many customers purchase items, and
- how they have designed the inside of their store.

An observant person could also find out how much an average transaction is by watching what customers are purchasing or by the amount displayed on the cash register's screen. Just remember that customers and sales tend to come in waves, so you may have to spend a little time there to really get an accurate idea.

All of these research tactics will help you decide if opening a store in the area is a good idea.

2.2 Ask potential customers

Besides finding out how many and what types of adult businesses are in the area, watch how frequently people shop at them. If there are a lot of adult boutiques operating in the area and you are not sure if there would be enough customers to turn a profit at a new adult retail store, the best way to

find this out would be to ask the potential customers. You can then more accurately decide if they would patronize your store as well as the others, if they would prefer to shop only at your new store, or if they would potentially like to shop at both.

If you feel you would be in direct competition with other adult stores in your area, it is even more imperative to set yourself apart from them and to listen to what your potential customers have to say about why they like or dislike the other stores. You can then create a competitive advantage over the other stores in numerous ways. For example, you could sell a larger or higher-end selection of lingerie, toys, shoes, or adult movies. You could create better marketing campaigns, merchandise your store better, have better prices or sales, carry a larger selection of brand-name items, or find a better location.

Conducting a general poll of adults that live in the area may prove very useful. If you cordially ask people to answer your opinion poll, they are generally happy to answer the questions because it makes them feel like someone cares about their opinions. However, as a friendly gesture (if you do not care if word gets round that you are interested in opening an adult store) you might want to offer these potential customers coupons for your upcoming store if they answer all of your questions. This gesture will make them feel like they are getting something for doing your poll and will provide them with a reminder of your store opening. The questions in your poll may include:

- "Would you be interested in shopping at an adult store in the area?" *This question would be best asked in an area where there are currently no adult stores, to gauge the interest of potential customers.*

- "Do you currently shop at an adult store in the area?" *If the customer responds to that question with a "yes," then it would be good to follow up with these questions:*

- "Which store do you frequent most often?"

- "What are your favorite things about the store?"

- "What are some of your favorite products?"

- "Do you think the pricing is fair?"

- "Do you like the business hours of the store?"

- "Is it the most popular store in town?"

- *If it is not the most popular store in town, you may want to ask:* "Where is the most popular store in town? Do you know people that shop there and why they might prefer that store?"

- "Would you prefer to shop at a different adult boutique in the area if you had the option?" *If they would rather shop at another store if given the choice, ask what improvements they would like to see at a new adult boutique.*

Keep in mind that when asking people about shopping in adult boutiques, they may only be able to imagine one type of store and would shop at a more classy store if they had any idea there was such a thing. Also note that they may not admit that they shop at adult stores, especially if there are other people around that could overhear them or if they feel that they would not remain anonymous.

2.3 Talk to owners of other adult boutiques

An easy way to find out more detailed information about other adult boutiques is to ask the owners. Sometimes store owners may be willing to tell you about their businesses if you ask them politely while complimenting their store. Most of the time, business owners feel flattered that another person is asking them questions about the store, so they are happy to talk about how it was first opened and how business is doing. This gives you the ability to ask questions and get answers that are specific to the area in which you will be operating your business. You may be pleasantly surprised at how much information a store owner will tell you just by asking.

2.4 Consider the indirect competition

It is easy to get caught thinking that the only stores you will be in competition with are other adult boutiques, but this is not necessarily the case. If you are planning on selling a lot of lingerie, you will have to set yourself apart from the large-chain lingerie retailers. These stores are beginning to realize that they can profit from selling more racy lingerie such as crotch-less panties and shelf bras, while still selling more classic-looking items.

Competition may come from other businesses as well as adult stores and specific lingerie stores. You will most likely be competing directly and indirectly with other large and small retailers. It may seem obvious to you who your competitors are, but often people underestimate other competition or do not think of all their potential competitors. Indirect competitors may be stores that only sell a few items that you sell in your store. For example, liquor stores sometimes sell adult movies, some large-chain drug stores sell sensual bath and body products (such as products from Kama Sutra®), Wal-Mart sells fishnet stockings and body jewelry, and grocery stores sell a large variety of personal lubricants and condoms.

Halloween stores are also major competitors for costume sales from the beginning of August through October. Halloween stores have become greater competitors every year in the sexy adult costume business. Remember the Halloween stores from a few years ago that sold mostly children's costumes and frumpy adult costumes? That time is long gone for most of them. Halloween stores are selling more sexy and racy costumes for adults every year.

The Internet is also being used more frequently as a vehicle to sell adult toys, adult movies, lingerie, and costumes. This may present serious competition for your store. Fortunately, some people still like to shop in brick-and-mortar stores because they can touch the product, try on clothing, and get customer assistance immediately. They also may not want to receive a package at their residence, or might simply not trust online shopping.

Although you may believe that your store is different from a liquor store, a grocery store, or the Internet, most customers will still compare your prices to them. You need to be aware of all of your competitors, because your customers certainly will be, and they will not want to spend more money on the same product if they know where to get it cheaper. Sometimes customers will pay a little bit more to shop in your store because you have a greater variety, you provide more privacy, or because of various other attributes that your customers like. However, if your prices are outrageously high compared to other places, be prepared to have fewer customers, which will make it harder to make a profit. Unless you are located in a ritzy area, most shoppers will not be willing to pay prices that are much higher than what they could pay somewhere else for similar items, even if it is more pleasant to shop in your store.

Always research as much information as you can about your competition and your potential customers. You will usually find that you missed something when you first thought about your customer market, and this could be a costly mistake. Do not assume that you know everything about your customers. For example, not all customers will want to shop for their personal products at a liquor store or grocery store, and not all customers will want to shop for lingerie at a discount store or on the Internet, but you cannot be fooled into thinking that these other places are not part of your competition. Instead of acknowledging only the obvious competitors, learn about other competition that may exist so that you can include them in your strategy to both gain and retain customers.

2.5 Zoning regulations

Finding a location can also be difficult because of zoning regulations. These are restrictions placed on where businesses are allowed to be and what type of businesses are allowed to be there. To find out the zoning laws, go to your city's zoning department and ask to get a zoning map. The map will tell you what the regulations are for each area of the city.

Refer to the city code on types of businesses if you are not sure of the laws pertaining to adult stores. It is easy to be misinformed so go directly to the source, as it is the easiest and most accurate way of finding out if your store would be considered an "adult store" or something similar. Sometimes you may find that you or other professionals at city hall are mistaken on what the laws actually are. With a little bit of research, you can arm yourself with some very helpful information when deciding whether to locate your business in one spot or another.

In my initial research on zoning regulations, I discovered that my store would not be considered an adult store. This is because more than 50 percent of the merchandise was not classified as "adult," but instead made up of lingerie, wigs, shoes, jewelry, and bath and body products, while slightly less than 50 percent of the merchandise consisted of adult toys, novelties, and DVDs. To be sure, I also asked the city attorney if there were any conflicting laws and was told that there were no laws against having the type of store I was about to set up in the location I had chosen. This ensured that there were no laws conflicting with my store plan.

2.6 Negotiating a commercial lease

Negotiating a commercial lease can be just as difficult as finding the right location. If you have never negotiated a commercial rental, you should learn more about it before you begin negotiating with the landlord. For more information on commercial leases, there are many great books on the subject, the Internet has some great sites, and Self-Counsel Press publishes a do-it-yourself CD-ROM entitled *Commercial Lease Agreements*. If you hired a commercial real estate agent to find you a location, he or she should also be able to inform you about commercial leases.

The following list includes some of the items most commonly negotiated in a commercial lease:

- Price per square foot.
- Time (duration) of the lease.
- Whether there are any renewal or extension terms when the lease ends.
- Who pays for major and minor building repairs.
- What happens to your lease if you are no longer in business. For example, will you be allowed to sublease and will the new tenant need to be approved by the landlord?

A commercial lease may seem daunting at first because of the amount of money you will be spending, and so you may not want to sign up for a long-term lease initially. However, if you believe that the location is an up-and-coming area or for some other reason believe that the rental rate will go up, it is to your advantage to sign a longer lease. This is especially true if you really like the spot and are sure you'll want to renew the lease.

When I set up shop, 40 percent of the businesses on my city block were vacant. In fact, one of my friends who was an advertising solicitor had said that it was a bad neighborhood to be in because all of her customers that were located in it had gone out of business. However, it was the only location available in the whole town after speaking with every commercial leaser in the city, and it did appear to be an up-and-coming area. Now the area has become a popular business location and the rent has gone up tremendously.

2.7 Moving an established business

If you have settled on a location, but you are not overly happy with it and plan to move the store someday, then you will need to consider what moving could do to your business. When your business starts to grow and you have spent a lot of money on advertising, it is very difficult to move and still keep all of your customers, as they may not want to travel to your new location or may not realize you have moved. You may not be able to find another location close to your old one either. Furthermore, if customers go into the new store that moved into your old location, they may spend all of their money there and not bother going to your new location (if it is a similar type of store or they like the new one more).

The lady who leased my commercial spot before I set up a business in it owned a women's retail boutique. She moved to a place a few blocks away more than six months before I set up my store. However, when my store opened, and even a year later, her customers continued coming into my store. I told the customers that the previous owner had moved, but many did not want to bother walking a few blocks to her store; they would spend their money in my store instead of going to the other newly located store. This shocked me at first because she did not move very far from her old spot, and her store sold different items. However, this shows how difficult it can be to move and keep your old customers.

3. The Pros and Cons of Buying an Established Business Versus Creating a New Business

There are good and bad things about purchasing an established adult store, as well as good and bad things about starting your own business. The decision to purchase a business versus creating a new one is highly dependent on your individual personality and needs. For example, you may or may not have a tolerance for risk, a fixed budget, or a high motivational drive. Since this decision is a very personal one, you will need to decide what is most important for you and what you are willing or able to deal with, and then base your decision on that. To assist you in making your decision, consider the main pros and cons of buying an existing business, as well as those for creating a new business.

3.1 Pros of buying an established business

One of the main pros of buying an established business is that the store will have an established clientele. Therefore, it will have an existing reputation and customer base. This means that it will have an immediate cash flow from these customers. A start-up company will need to build up its client base before it can have a substantial and reliable cash flow.

The financial documents of an established business can be examined to find out what financial position you can reasonably expect to be in once you purchase the business. Some of the important facts you would be able to deduce from the financial documents would include:

- Cash flow (how large and reliable it would be).

- Expenditures.

- Profit margin.

- Seasonal fluctuations (if you are provided with monthly financial statements as well as annual ones).

If needed, outside financing might be easier to obtain. The loaner will be able to assess the performance track record of the existing store, and base their lending decision on that.

Often, vendors will provide discounts, fill orders more quickly, or give other preferential treatment to long-term customers. The store might already have these discounts available and the vendors will most likely pass them on to the new owner.

Another pro when buying an established store is that the business might already have one of the best locations in town. Since the store already exists, you will know if there has been any controversy over the adult store and what the complaints of the city or community are. Also, the store will have established employees that are knowledgeable about the products currently stocked.

By buying an established store, your energy can be spent focusing on improving the current business versus starting from scratch. Dealing with start-up expenses and the many other things involved in beginning a new business may be a lot more work than going into an already established business (if the business is doing well).

You will be purchasing a store that would have been a competitor if you had decided to start a store in the same area as the already-established one. Therefore, you will have less direct store competition. Often a noncompetition clause is included in the sale contract of the business. Generally, the previous owner will not be allowed to start a new, similar type of business, help to create one, or work as a manager in one within a specified perimeter of the existing business, for a certain time period after the sale. Therefore, there will also be less competition from the former owner in the near future.

3.2 Cons of buying an established business

The up-front cost of purchasing an established business is almost always higher than the cost of creating a new business. A seller might want to sell his or her tangible assets such as furniture, fixtures, equipment, and inventory for more than market value. Also, a seller usually expects to receive added monetary compensation included in the sale price for *goodwill*, and other intangible assets of value to the company, such as any related trademarks and copyrights the owner might hold. Goodwill is the price the owner has calculated for things such as the time, effort, risk, money it took him or her to generate the current customer base (i.e, the money spent on advertising), and other things that made the business the way it currently is. In general, the amount of goodwill should reflect the value of the store's customer base.

If you are considering buying an established business you will need to look closely at the financial statements of the company. The financial statements might be biased, incomplete, or inaccurate.

Depending on how your sale contract is written, you can inherit all of the known and unknown liabilities of the existing business. This could include all unpaid bills; any current, pending, or future lawsuits as a result of an action from the previous store owner; and gift certificate and credit memos held by customers. Even if your sale contract excludes these liabilities, there may be laws or other loopholes in the contract that could still hold you liable for these debts. Even if your contract is legally sound and loophole proof, there still might be obstacles to overcome. For example, you may upset customers by not honoring vouchers that they received from the previous owner, or vendors might not want to do business with the store if there are unpaid bills from the previous owner.

The previous owner might not have had good relations with some of its vendors. There may be vendors that refuse to do business with the store because of the previous owner's unfair demands, chronic late payments, decisions to charge a different price to customers than the manufacturer's suggested price, or for other reasons.

The previous owner might not have had good relations with some of its customers as well. Therefore, there might be a group of jilted customers that you are unaware of. These customers may not want to shop at the store anymore and they might have made up a large portion of the previous sales.

There might have been a lot of customers coming into the store because they liked the original owner. When the original owner leaves, these customers may decide to shop at a different store if they do not like you or your new policies.

Another challenge may be the current store employees; they may be unsatisfied with their jobs, they may not like the change of ownership, or they may simply not want to follow any new changes you implement. New changes are hard to avoid and might include: current pay or pay scale changes, sick leave or vacation time for employees, store policies for customers and/or employees, acceptable behavior guidelines for employees, and in general, the way you operate the business.

You will also need to consider the surrounding neighborhood, road infrastructure, and other things that may affect your store location. For example, the neighborhood might be entering an economic slump or there might be plans to build a freeway that would make the current road to the store inaccessible.

You will need to check the lease terms. For example, the lease on the building might be expiring and the owner of the building might want to sell it, charge significantly more rent, or the current business out of its location once the lease has expired.

There also might not be a lot of adult stores for sale in the area you would like to purchase one. Even if there are several adult businesses for sale in the area, you may not find one you would be happy owning. Therefore, if you are seeking to buy an existing adult business, you will most likely be confined to owning one in a certain area, and owning one that might not fit all of the criteria you were looking for.

The final downside to purchasing an already established business may be that the feeling of achievement obtained from creating a new business will not exist. Therefore, it may be harder to take ownership pride in the new business.

3.3 Pros of creating a business

One of the biggest pros of starting a new business is that the up-front cost is usually much less than the cost of purchasing an existing business because there is no goodwill payment.

Another advantage to creating your own store is that you can pick your store location anywhere — withstanding legal and vacancy restraints. It also means that you

should be able to create the type of store you want to own, such as a WCF or adult video store.

Starting your own store from scratch means that there will be no existing business liabilities for the store. It also means that there cannot be any unhappy customers, disgruntled employees, unsatisfied vendors, or other people (e.g., business neighbors) who are displeased with the store.

The best thing about starting a business is that you can use your creativity and skills to start a business from scratch and do it your own way. The ownership pride and sense of fulfillment and achievement for you may be much higher as a result.

3.4 Cons of creating a business

One of the cons of creating a business is that there is no financial history on which to base any of your decisions. There is huge risk in putting money, time, and effort into the project when you cannot guarantee your rate of return. It will also take time to establish a customer base and therefore start receiving a reliable cash flow.

It can be complicated to judge how much money you will need to open your business and keep it running until you start to make a profit. Therefore, you might end up undercapitalized and may have to skimp on materials, advertising, or other aspects of the business. It is hard to plan your life around an uncertain monetary income. Also, it is difficult to know exactly how much time and effort you will be spending creating a new store. Typically, a business owner starting a new store spends hundreds of hours and a lot of his or her own money when starting the business. The business failure rate for new, start-up companies is higher than for existing businesses.

You will not yet have staff for your business. Therefore, you will not have anyone to help you start the business until you find people (if you are planning on hiring employees) and there will be no one to cover during any sick, vacation, or other time you take off.

If you have another job, you will most likely need to quit your job sooner if you start your own company than if you purchased one, due to the time you will need to invest in starting it. Thus, the cost of starting a new business will be higher.

It is easy to lose motivation, get distracted, or lose sight of your goals when creating a company. There are a lot of small details and milestones to accomplish before you can begin to visually see a retail store, and this can be difficult for people without a lot of vision for the future or dedication to the end result.

4. Be Proud of the Type of Store and Location That You Choose

The type of customers that will come into your store will depend on the type of store you have. The more competition among adult stores in your area, the more choices people will have and the more segregated your shoppers will become according to their tastes and budgets. If you like dealing with more women and couples, then having a women- and couple-friendly store would be more appropriate for you. This would require more personal attention than other adult stores. For example, you would have to deal with couples who would like to spice up their love lives, ladies who ask you which products could help them get their first orgasms, or older couples who want to know how to work around their medical problems. If this sounds like pesky business to you, owning an adult store that will attract more of a rough or male-only crowd is your best bet!

Which type of adult store you would be most comfortable operating, and which you would benefit the most from financially, are equally important considerations. You could find that the type of store you want to own may not be the most profitable option. However, there are ways to work around these problems. For example, if you are determined to own a store that you do not think would benefit you financially, start seeking ways in which to make it more profitable (such as differentiating your store from others in the area or opening your store in another area of the city). If you decide that profitability of the business is the only important issue, remember that it may become increasingly difficult to put energy into running the business when you do not enjoy doing it, and that the venture may suffer as a result. Owning a store that you are proud of will likely enable you to want to work harder at making it a great and profitable business venture.

3
DEVELOP A BUSINESS PLAN

A business plan is an essential tool to help you organize your business and make the right decisions for your company, by forcing you to think about what you are doing and write it down on paper.

A business plan will help you plan your business strategy at the start, and help guide your business into a profitable future. Writing a business plan may sound like a lot of hard, tedious work, but it will help you to stay focused on your goal and carry out what is necessary to ensure your success, and it will encourage you to have realistic expectations. Developing a business plan will help you create a more successful business!

A business plan will help you figure out and organize what you need to do to get your business started on the right track, and it will also help you plan what your business will be like years from now.

If you need financing, a business plan may be a necessary tool to convince a bank or investors to loan you money. A well-thought-out and realistic business plan will also assist you in obtaining loans and credit from vendors. Setting down your ideas and goals in a business plan shows people that you know what you are doing and how you are going to go about implementing your plans. A business plan should not only convince other people that you will create a profitable business, it should also convince you that you have made the correct choice as to what type of store you are opening and that the timing is right for you to run your own store.

Some people are afraid of creating a business plan because they are worried that it may prove to them that opening the business they have always dreamed of is not actually a good idea. The business plan may

29

show that the business would not be profitable, or highlight some other reasons for concern. However, it is always best to figure this out before you spend the cash and realize that you have made the wrong decision to own a own business.

Even if you already have a business plan formulated in your head, writing it down will enable you to find ways to make the business even more profitable, to come up with new ideas, or to change your plan for the better.

There are many different ways to write a business plan, but most of them follow the same general points as they all serve the same purpose — to make the business profitable. Your business plan should answer the following ten questions:

1. What do you want your business to accomplish?

2. What are your qualifications to run the business?

3. Who will perform the work?

4. What is your marketing plan?

5. How will the business be financed?

6. How much will it cost to start and run the store?

7. Are you willing and able to spend the money in order for it to become a profitable business?

8. Will the store make money and how long will this take?

9. How much profit are you expecting?

10. What will the business be like three to five years from now?

These ten questions may seem very easy to answer, but most people do not thoroughly think them through before they start their own business. Not doing so has often led to disaster for many small-business owners. Unfortunately, most small businesses fail. People get excited about owning their own business but they often don't realize the amount of work they need to put into it, or they fail to predict all of the costs. It may sound stupid, but it is easy to forget about advertising or keeping your accounting records organized when it gets extremely hectic!

A business plan must be well written. In other words, there should be no typographical or grammatical errors. It should have headings to describe the different sections of the plan so the reader can go to the section he or she is most interested in reading. If it contains many pages, then a table of contents can also benefit the reader. If you need to show your business plan to potential investors, a professionally-written plan will be more influential than one that is poorly written.

1. The Business Plan

The following sections outline what you should include in your business plan.

1.1 Executive summary

An executive summary is an introductory summary of the entire business plan. It should give the reader a general outline by providing a one- to two-sentence synopsis of each section of the business plan. Every important issue should be mentioned in the summary; leave the details of these issues for when the entire document is read. Although the executive summary goes at the beginning of the business plan, the summary is usually the last part that you write and is usually no more than one page in length.

Often the executive summary will be tailored to the intended reader, and what they will think are the most important aspects. For example, if you are preparing the business plan to show to a loan agent, you would focus on the projected finances of the company, but if you were going to show it to a city official, you would focus on the description and location of the business.

1.2 The mission statement

The next section of your business plan is the mission statement. Your mission statement will explain what your business is trying to accomplish. It is usually concise, with no more than one or two sentences. For example, the following mission statement is the one we wrote for my company:

To provide retail products in a clean, friendly environment that promotes romance and healthy sexuality.

Another example of a mission statement is the following one for Limited Brands, which is the company that owns Victoria's Secret:

Limited Brands is committed to building a family of the world's best fashion brands offering captivating customer experiences that drive long-term loyalty and deliver sustained growth for our shareholders.

The mission statement for your company should allow you and anybody else involved in the business to have a common understanding and goal regarding what the company should be working toward.

1.3 History and background

Investors, business advisers, banks, and other people with money or time invested in your business will want to feel certain that you have the ambition, dedication, and skills to create a profitable business. These people will not want to invest in something they believe will never become fruitful. A good way to demonstrate that it will is to show them that you have a history of the characteristics and the credentials necessary to create a valuable business.

In the history and background section of your business plan you should describe how your qualifications will enable you to successfully run the business. If you have worked at or managed an adult boutique, describe the skills from your previous job that you will use to make your business profitable. If you have never worked in an adult boutique, but you have experience owning or running another retail outlet, describe how the skills from this job transfer to the new business. If you have a college or university degree in business management, for example, then describe it in this section and explain how it will support your business plans.

You want your ambition, dedication, and skills to show that you are able and willing to do hard work and put in the time necessary to follow through with your goals. Writing a synopsis of your accomplishments, along with an explanation of why you would like to own your own business, is an excellent way to show people what you would like to accomplish in the future, that you are serious about your work, and that you have a history of being able to accomplish your dreams.

1.4 Description of your business

In this section, you will be defining your business. After reading this section the reader should have a clear understanding of what the business will be like. In other words, he or she should be able to identify how your store is similar to other stores, and how it would differ. Here you should discuss the name of your business, the industry your business will be in, the specific type of business you will operate within this industry, and the location of the store.

The name of your business is very important and warrants extra attention. This is where you would talk about it in detail. You should include why you chose the name and how it will attract customers. It is usually one of the first pieces of information customers will learn about your store, and provides them with a way to identify it.

By this point, you should have decided which section of the industry your business will take part in. Provide a general definition of the industry and then explain in further detail what the climate of the industry is like and how this will affect your business. The climate includes:

- The popularity of the industry.

- Whether the industry is growing or stressed and shrinking.

- The type of competitors in the industry and how many competitors there are.

- How many vendors there are in the industry.

- Whether the industry generally accepts newcomers.

- What types of resources you will have.

- What types of regulations you will have to abide by.

Next, explain in detail the exact type of business you plan to operate within this industry. There are two major points in this decision:

- Who will the store be designed for?

- What types of products and/or services will you sell?

Begin by writing descriptions of your target customers such as their gender and class, whether they are single or married, if they will shop alone or with other people, or other distinguishing features that characterize them. Then, discuss the categories and quality of products your store will be selling, and any services your store might provide. These two aspects should lead the reader to your conclusion as to whether the store is an adult video store, adult bookstore, or a women- and couple-friendly (WCF) store (as discussed in Chapter 2).

It will be helpful if the reader can envision how you will obtain your products and carry out any services the store might offer (such as adult toy parties or classes). You might want to discuss in general how you will choose your vendors and any outside agencies you are going to hire. More detailed information on the operations side of your business will need to be discussed under the "operations and employees" section of your business plan, which is discussed later in section **1.6**.

Most likely, your business will be affected by your location, due to the type of customers shopping in the area and the products and/or services you are legally allowed to sell. If you already have a location for your business, you should discuss its pros and cons. If you do not have one yet, you can discuss where you would prefer to have your store, what the possible locations are, and why you think these places are beneficial for the store and its customers. If you plan on having an online store, you will discuss if it will differ from your retail store or be an extension of it, and how you will run the website (including how you will operate and advertise the website).

1.5 Company values

Your company's values should serve as a guide for its conduct. If the values are embraced by everyone in the company they will shape and define the business's character. This character plays a large role in employee relations and customer relations, and can be used as a marketing tool if customers share these values.

Defining a company's values is similar to defining a person's own values. The only difference is that you will try to make the entire organization, management, and staff act in accordance with this set of values.

The responses to the groups of questions below should help guide you in defining your company's values. The questions will help you come up with your own ideas of what a company's values should encompass.

Company self-worth:

- Will you take pride in your company?
- Is the company policy to be honest at all times?

- What kind of overall impression would you like the company to make on the community, its customers, and its employees?

Customers:

- How will you treat your customers?
- Will you try to get to know your customers?
- Will you ever turn away potential customers?
- How will you deal with different types of customers?
- Will you constantly look for ways to improve customer service?

Employees:

- Are your employees an important part of your company?
- Will you take the time to listen to your employees' needs?
- What sort of values will you trying to instill in your employees?

Business-to-business relations:

- What values will you use in dealing with your vendors?
- What values do you expect your vendors to have?

Community relations:

- Do you care about the community and how it will react to your store?
- Will you try and mitigate any fears the community has about your store?
- How far are you willing to go to satisfy each community member's concerns with your store?

- Are you going to be active in the community and in community events?

- How will your business benefit the community?

Environmental impact:

- Are there any major environmental issues that could cause concern for your business?

- Will you do your best to recycle and use recyclable products in your business?

- Will you prevent paper waste and waste of other administrative office supplies?

1.6 Operations and employees

The organizational management and employee structure of your company will dictate how your store will operate. You will need to decide how you want to create this structure. The following points suggest different ways you can organize your human resources.

- Have an independent manager with a lot of decision-making power and control.

- Have a shift manager that only manages shift work and does not make major decisions.

- Be the only manager and just have employees.

- Operate the store completely by yourself with no employees.

- Operate the store yourself except during holidays when you will hire seasonal workers.

If you decide to hire employees, having a clear picture of what you need them to do will help you figure out what type and how many managers and employees you will need. The qualities, skills, past experience, and other related résumé criteria you will require of them should support the values of the company.

The amount and type of managers and employees you will hire will also help you decide on your store's hours of operation. For example, if you have decided to do everything yourself, it is unlikely that you will be able to work more than ten hours a day each day of the week. On the other hand, if you have decided to hire multiple managers and employees, you might not have to be present at the store very often.

Remember that the hours of operation are not always the same as the store hours. If you plan on restocking items or doing administrative work before or after store hours, this adds to the total number of hours your store will be operating.

1.7 Market research

Never underestimate your competition, as this can easily lead to a huge loss in customers. If you do not take enough time to carefully research and analyze your competitors, you will almost certainly run into this problem. Therefore, this section should be devoted to explaining what research you have done, who your competition is, what they are like, and what your store's competitive advantage is. See Chapter 2 for more information about researching the competition.

Start by describing your direct and indirect research methods for finding out who your competitors are and where they are located. Your direct research methods will include those that you did first hand (for example, you drove through the neighbourhoods to locate them). Your indirect research methods should describe how you researched other people's first-hand information (for example, if you looked in phone directories or on the Internet).

The next step is to list your competition and describe what type of competitors they are. Do they present direct or indirect competition? In other words, would you classify these stores as being in the same type of industry or do they simply sell some of the same products you will be selling? Based on this information, try to assess how big their impact will be on your store.

Then describe what each of these stores has to offer its customers and how you researched this information. In your description, you should include the answers to the following questions:

- How far away are these stores from your location?

- What community do you think they serve?

- Do they have an Internet site or other store locations?

- What products do they carry and how are they priced?

- How do they advertise?

- Do they provide customer service?

An important part of creating your store is making sure it has a competitive advantage over its competition. This means that your store will do better than its competitors.

Use the information you have gathered to help you determine how to entice potential customers to shop at your store versus your competitors'. Describe how you will do this. For example, will you offer your customers a greater selection of products at a better price, will you have a higher standard of customer service, or will you have a better location or longer store hours?

You should also try to assess what your future competition will be like and how your company will stay ahead of it. Explain how you think the industry might be changing and how this will affect the number of competitors you will have. Assess how your current and future competitors may affect your market share. Also, discuss how you anticipate the market for your products and services will change.

Discuss additional ways in which you will keep abreast of your competition and how often you will do any necessary work to find out more details about them. If you stay aware of what your competitors are doing on a daily basis, they are less likely to catch you off guard and leave your store in the dust. There are many ways to keep abreast of your competition without doing too much work. For example, keep your eyes and ears open for any advertising in local newspapers, on TV, on the radio, or in other types of media you normally watch or listen to. Pay attention to your customers. Customers will often compare your store to similar types of stores. When you are out doing your own personal shopping, take notice of stores that might be nudging into your market share by selling items similar to those you sell.

1.8 Sales and marketing strategy

Your sales and marketing strategy should provide a detailed description of how you will get and maintain your customers. Your description should include how you will market your business, what types of advertising you will use, the sales techniques your salespeople will use once your customers are in the store, and any other means you use to achieve this.

First you will need to discuss the characteristics you want your customers to associate with your store. Decide whether you want your store to be well known for providing customer service, quality products, the latest styles, or some other positive aspect. After you have done this, focus on how you will get potential customers to associate your business with these benefits.

You will need to come up with a marketing plan to spread your good reputation. Write about all of the ways in which you are going to influence your business's outreach. These may include: whether you will have a liaison with any community, business, or charity groups; if you will write short articles about your store and submit them to the local newspapers or other community-type mailers; and if you will host an event at the store such as a grand opening.

The next step is to write about how you will advertise the business through flyers, newspapers, radio spots, the Internet, or other means. You should include detail about where you will advertise, how your advertisements will look, how large they will be, how much you are going to spend on them, and what target audience you will be advertising to. By contacting advertising sources and asking them about their pricing structure, you can obtain a basic advertising rate information card. This will provide you with a better idea of costs and will therefore help you to create a realistic advertising plan.

Last but not least, describe a sales strategy that will guide you and your employees when providing customer service and selling products. It would be helpful to list the sales techniques that you will use and the reasons you think they will work. For example, knowledge of all the accessories that go with a particular product will help you up-sell these items. Chapter 10 will provide you with detailed information on sales strategy techniques.

1.9 Financial plan

Besides pride of ownership and independence, the reason most people want to own their own business is to make money. Therefore, one of the most important things you will want to calculate is how much profit your business could generate. Of course, there is no crystal ball that is going to tell you exactly how much money you will make, but you can at least approximate a realistic figure.

The financial plan is the main part of your business plan and you should spend the most time developing this section. If you are trying to convince a bank to lend you money or to get people to invest in your business, you must be able to show them that your business and financial plans are going to make the venture profitable.

The three main financial statements of a company are the Income Statement (or Profit and Loss Statement), the Balance Sheet, and the Cash-Flow Statement. They are usually prepared on a monthly, quarterly, and annual basis. Creating them should give you a good idea of the general amount of money you will be making and how long it will take you to pay off your debts. Your lenders will usually want to see projected figures for these documents. Some will require more detailed information than others, but most lenders want at least some general predictions as to how much your business will make so that they can approximate when they will be making a return on their investment.

The Income Statement provides you with the net income of your store by subtracting your total revenue from the cost of sales and expenses. Creating a projected Income Statement for a company that has not yet been created means that you will need to do some research on the numbers to include. For example, to figure out projected revenues, seek advice from other professionals in the same industry (such as other owners), or research trade association articles. For cost of sales, call vendors to find out about pricing. For expenses, call the companies where you will be spending money and ask them what their prices are and how much a business your size will usually spend.

This is the main document used to project if the store will make money, so everyone investing in your company will want to see it. For a more detailed description of how to predict these numbers, please see Chapter 4, section **2**.

The Balance Sheet is the document that shows you how much the company is worth from the perspective of its total liabilities and assets. Included in this statement is everything the company owns and all of its debts. If you are interested in taking on loans and other types of financing, this is where you will project how much you will owe and how long it will take you to pay it back. Your loan agent or anyone else interested in providing you with start-up money will want to know how much of your own money you are preparing to stake in your company and if there are any other people you will need to pay back.

Lastly, your Cash-Flow Statement tracks where your money is coming from and where it's going. This statement will let you know if you will have money when you need it. For example, it will tell you if you have enough money to pay your bills.

These financial statements will help you explain how you will make money and acquire financing for start-up costs, and will predict how long you think it will take before the store begins to make a profit. They will also help you determine how much of your own money you will spend in order to get the store up and running.

You may want to hire a financial planner to help you figure out the details of your financial plan.

1.10 Forecasts and projections

A forecast of how your business will perform in the future will help you plan for how to get there. The forecast for your business should read like a road map from Point A (right now) to Point B (sometime in the future) and include all of the pit stops in the middle. The pit stops are the points where you can stop and assess if you are on the right road heading where you want to go, or if you need to change directions to get back on course.

Figuring out where you want your company to be three to five years from now will help you determine its progression from Point A to Point B. For example, if you want to grow your company 100 percent in the next 5 years, you will need to plan for the expansion by setting aside money for the company's growth.

By creating a business plan at the beginning that outlines your company's future, you will have a document that you can habitually revisit to see if you are progressing toward your goals. If, after the first year, you revisit your plan and discover you are off track, you can correct your course.

Without having an idea of where you want your business to be in the future, it is hard to properly plan how to get there. Without planning, you might be stuck without enough money to grow your company, or you might have a completely different company than you initially anticipated. Perhaps your customer base is not what you had hoped.

Decide what you want your business to accomplish in the short-term future. Making a list of your goals will help you focus on how you want to shape and grow your business and what actions you need to take in order to get there.

Some examples of possible short- and long-term goals are listed below to provide you with ideas of what the goals for your company may include.

Short-term goals (within one year):

- Create a reward system for customers.
- Implement a commission-based structure for employees.

- Start advertising in additional newspapers.
- Join a trade association group.
- Partner with local businesses.
- Start saving for an additional location.

Long-term goals (within two to five years):

- Increase annual sales by 20 percent each year.
- Start donating to local charity groups.
- Upgrade furniture and fixtures.
- Open a new location.

Creating a budget will assist you in saving for whichever goals you are setting that will require money, such as wanting to give your employees a holiday bonus or opening a new location. To prepare a budget, take your gross sales and subtract all of your expenses including cost of goods sold. If you have added in all of the items that you will need to save money for, your budget will show you whether your goals are financially feasible.

2. Revisiting Your Business Plan

Revisiting your business plan quarterly will keep it fresh in your mind and help guide you toward achieving the goals you set. A good way to make sure you are revisiting the plan is to have a time picked out when you will review it. For example, revisit the business plan each time you review your quarterly business statements.

Keeping your business plan fresh in your mind is important in ensuring that you are on track and moving towards the goals and objectives you set. In an effort to do this, companies will sometimes post parts of their business plan (such as their mission statement) in an obvious place where employees can view it every day.

You should revisit your business plan before each major change, such as when you revise the budget or open a new location, or when new competitors open a store. Your business plan will remind you what is most important and will help guide you when making decisions for the company.

3. Get a Professional's Opinion on the Business

It is a good idea to get a professional's opinion about your business before you open your doors to the public. There are professionals who can help you with a multitude of different business start-up topics. For example, a professional can make suggestions for improving your business plan, remind you of something in the setup of your business that you have forgotten, or recommend where to take business classes if you feel you need them.

Often, there are local business offices designated to helping entrepreneurs start new businesses in the local community. Ask your city hall where you might be able to find business start-up assistance in the area.

The US Small Business Administration (SBA) can also be of assistance in obtaining information on starting a business. The SBA was created specifically to assist small-business owners in the USA. You can contact the SBA by calling 1-800-U-ASK-SBA toll-free, or by visiting www.sba.gov. If there isn't an SBA office located near you, they will assist you in finding a regional business agency that can help you with your start-up needs.

Canadians can contact Canada Business, which provides services for Canadian entrepreneurs, by calling 1-888-576-4444 toll-free, or by visiting www.canadabusiness.ca.

4

CONSIDER THE COSTS OF STARTING A BUSINESS

Starting your own business can be very expensive, and spending a lot more money than you normally do can be daunting. After you have decided that spending the money and time on your new venture is worth it, decide whether or not you will be able to afford it.

1. Finance Your Business

Financing your business may be difficult and may affect the type of business structure (e.g., sole proprietorship, partnership, corporation, or limited liability company) that you choose. Decide which business structure would be best for you and then look into how you can finance it. Knowing which type of business you would like to have first will ensure that you don't compromise your venture by taking on ill-suited partners or meddling corporate investors if you don't have to. However, obtaining enough capital to start your business right can sometimes be difficult. For more information about business structures see Chapter 5.

There are two general categories of financing that are most commonly used by businesses: equity financing and debt financing. If you have both options, figure out which financing structure is best for your individual personality, and from where you would be willing to accept financing. You should ask yourself the following questions:

- If you take on a partner and he or she does not work as hard or as intelligently as you, will it continuously annoy you to share all of the profits with him or her?

- Will you be able to handle someone else having the right to partake in decision-making for the company?

- Could you live with the fact that you could lose your family members' money if the company does not perform well financially?

Unfortunately, there is no crystal ball that will tell you which option is best for you and your company. Gathering as many options as you can, so you can make an informed decision and choose the financing structure that is best for you and your company, can be an essential and enjoyable part of creating a profitable business.

1.1 Equity financing

Equity financing happens when people put money into the company in order to own a part or all of the business. Since the money is given to the company through people expecting to own part of it, you must be willing to give part of your decision-making power to these outside investors. Make sure that the participants understand the amount of decision-making power they will have in the company's affairs and that you are willing to accept that they may not always be as good a business partner as you would like them to be.

Equity financing is most commonly obtained by seeking angel investors, venture capital, business partners, shareholders, stockholders, or having family and/or friends invest in your company. This option should

be very well-thought-out before you choose it because it may cost you more money and grief in the future. For example, you might become stuck with a corporate investor that has completely different goals for the company than you do or you might become stuck with an incompatible partner. Additionally, the investor will own a piece of the company, so you will be continuously paying them for their share no matter how much the business earns and grows.

1.2 Debt financing

Debt financing is money that a business receives as a loan. This means that the person giving the money does not own any of the business, but receives interest along with his or her money back. The advantage of this type of financing is that once you pay it back, you are free and clear of any future payments. The downside is that you will be required to make payments to the lender even if your business is not generating any profit (whereas with equity financing, you usually only have to make payouts from your profits).

Since debt financing comes from people or companies that lend money but do not own any part of your business, lenders do not have any decision-making abilities. Debt financing may take the form of personal credit card debt, home equity loans, government or commercial loans, or loans from family and/or friends that do not want to have any ownership in the company. With debt financing, the people and companies loaning the money receive interest along with the repayment of their loan, as their fee for loaning the money. To offset the cost of this interest, the business owner is usually allowed to write it off on the company's tax returns.

1.3 Obtain financing

After considering and researching all of your financing options, choose the one that is best for you and then start the process of acquiring it. This step may take longer than you realize, or longer than your financier originally indicated.

The way you go about securing financing will depend on how you have chosen to finance your company. Some of the ways in which you could begin the search for financing are listed below:

- Ask people you know who are interested in your start-up if they would like to invest in your company. If so, discuss with them how much they would be willing to invest and at what price.

- Submit your business plan to venture capital firms and/or angel investors that invest in your type of business. You can research these companies and investors by using online venture capital directories, and then check out firms' individual websites for more information.

- Check with your mortgage company or other financial service companies, to find out if you are eligible for a home equity line of credit.

- Go to banks specializing in business loans and speak with the loan agents about your options.

- Find out about any government loans by inquiring with the US Small Business Administration or Canada Business.

- Attend classes on how to obtain financing for small businesses. These are sometimes provided by local colleges, libraries, or community centers.

2. Start-up and Operational Costs

After you have decided that there is a market for your products, you will want to calculate how much it will cost to open the store and operate the store each day. Most importantly, you will want to know if your operating costs exceed your predicted or reasonable daily sales. Even if you are certain you will have a lot of customers, you may be shocked at how much you actually have to sell in order to cover the cost of operating the store while still taking home a profit.

The first time start-up costs of opening your own business can vary greatly. This cost can be tremendously different depending on several factors, such as whether you shop around for your fixtures, furniture, equipment, and other items, and whether you hire people to assist you in setting up your store. You will also need to factor in the cost of quitting another job to give yourself time to prepare, open, and run your adult store. The good news is that you will not incur these costs again after you purchase the start-up items and open the store, so the business's income should begin to offset the financial void from leaving another job.

Tip: To find the best deals on items you need to buy for your store, try looking around on the Internet and in phone directories for used furniture and fixture stores.

When you estimate how much capital you will need to start your business, include enough money to pay all of the business's expenses for the first three to six months. You may need more money than you originally thought, as your business could fail to turn a profit for several months or more, and you will still need to pay your business's bills and your personal expenses.

In order to figure out how fast you can recuperate your initial start-up capital, you will need to subtract your daily operating costs from your sales, then subtract any profit that you need to take home as income. The remainder could then be used to pay yourself back. The first step in figuring out how much it will cost to operate the store is to come up with a daily operating cost analysis. A daily operating cost analysis should include the following expenses:

- Cost of goods sold

- Commercial lease for the building

- Advertising

- Utilities (e.g., gas, electricity, water, sewer, garbage, phone, fax, and Internet access)

- Security system fees

- Building and inventory insurance

- Business licenses and other licenses, such as software for the point of sale system (unless you decide to use a cash register)

- Credit card and bank fees

- Accounting and bookkeeping fees (and possibly other professional fees)

- Office expenses (e.g., cash register paper, ink, paper, pens and pencils, price tags, postage, etc.)

- Store decorations

- Regular maintenance for the building and equipment

If you decide to hire employees, you will also have to consider the following fees:

- Employee wages

- Payroll expenses (e.g., wages and taxes)

- Employee benefits

- Insurance (e.g., building and business insurance, and employee injury insurance)

You also need to consider the cost of inventory shrinkage due to theft by customers and potentially by employees.

Depending on how you are going to finance your business, you may also need to think about finance and interest charges on your loan. It is easy to become overwhelmed thinking about all of these fees, but it is in your best interest to be as educated as possible about your venture, so you know if it is possible to make a profit before you start the business. Take one step at a time and start by calling the appropriate agencies and asking them if they can give you an approximation of the amount of money most businesses of your size pay for these services.

As you will figure out, all of these daily costs can add up. For example, utility fees such as garbage and electricity are most likely going to be higher than the fees you pay at home, because utility companies generally charge businesses more than they charge individuals. To find out the cost of these expenses, call the companies that provide the services and ask them to approximate the cost.

Research the going rate for rent in the area in which you would like to locate your store to give yourself a more accurate idea of how much you will need to pay for store space. This will also give you something to go on when negotiating with any future landlord.

3. The Importance of Paying Vendors and Suppliers

Another reason you need to make sure you have enough cash when you open the store is to ensure that you can pay your vendors and suppliers in a timely manner. The last thing you need is to create problems with your vendors right from the start, because you do not have enough money to pay them. Not being able to pay one of your major suppliers can be a costly mistake, because the supplier can always decide that they do not want your store as one of their customers and then you will not be able to buy the merchandise you need to sell.

If you are not paying your bills on time, it could also ruin your personal credit (if you are a self-proprietor) or your business's credit, which could hinder you and/or your business's chances of obtaining credit in the future.

4. Calculate Your Profits

It is easy for people to get caught up in the belief that owning their own business means making a lot of money. However, the majority of start-up businesses fail during the first three years because they are not making enough profit or the owners are burnt out from the amount of time they spend at work.

Not all business owners bother to figure out how much profit they can realistically make from owning their own venture. It can be extremely hard on business owners when they realize that owning a business can be a lot of hard work and long hours, and may not be as profitable as they believed it would be. In reality, most store owners do not make a lot of money and they spend more time on their business than they had expected. Coming up with an approximate, realistic prediction of the amount of profit your store will bring in, and then asking yourself if spending the money and time on the business is worth it, can save you a lot of money, time, and heartache!

Therefore, it is important to predict as accurately as possible how much profit you believe the store will make and how much time you will need to spend to achieve this profit, then evaluate whether these predictions sound acceptable to you.

Using all of the information that you have gathered, you can begin to calculate how much it will cost to run the store. First, write down how much you believe that your store can make in sales on an average day. For example, from watching how busy other adult stores are, you may have guessed that you can make about $800 in net sales on an average day. Of course, you will have holiday months, such as February, October, and December, in which adult "couples" stores will definitely have higher sales. However, months such as January, March, and November will be slower. So do not go into other stores on October 23 or December 24 and think that their stores are always that busy!

You will also need to calculate your expenses so that you can predict the amount of money in sales you'll need on an average day to break even. This is a good number to keep in mind, because all sales beyond the break-even point will be your profit after you have subtracted the cost of goods sold. To calculate the break-even point, take your estimated daily cost of doing business and divide it by your markup. For example, if your average cost of goods sold is 40 percent of the sale price, then your markup is 60 percent and you would divide your cost of doing business by 0.6 to come up with your break-even sale point. If the cost of doing business is $400 per day and you have a 60 percent average markup, then your approximate break-even point is $666.67.

If you were open six days a week and averaged $800 a day, sales would be $4,800 a week. Sales for a month would be $19,200. If you subtract the cost of goods from this equation (about 40 percent), it would be $11,520. Now calculate what all your expenses would cost on a monthly basis and subtract the expenses from $11,520. You would then have an idea of how much running your business would cost, and a prediction of how much profit you might realize.

It takes a little extra time to calculate this, but wouldn't you rather know how profitable your store might be, rather than to find out that all of your work was not as profitable as you had originally thought?

5
Taking the Appropriate Steps

Accomplishing all of the legal and business tasks necessary to start your own business can be very difficult. This is because there are so many different things that need to get done, and some things might take longer than you anticipated. One of the best ways to make sure that you complete it all is to get organized! Make a list of all of the things that need to be done and set deadlines for task completion. This chapter will outline some of the decisions you need to make and the realities you can expect to encounter when starting your business.

1. Business Name

Your business name should be well thought through. A name is what will help your customers identify your store. Therefore,

you want to make sure that whenever your customer comes into contact with the name visually or verbally, it will mean something to them and will be memorable.

Sure, there are some major stores with names that make it difficult to distinguish what they sell, or perhaps the names are hard to spell, but these stores have humongous advertising budgets and therefore are able to ingrain the important information about the store into their customers' heads with the volume and length of their marketing campaigns. Most likely, however, you will own a small- to medium-sized company to begin with. Therefore, choose a name that tells or strongly insinuates what you sell so that the customer does not need a lengthy explanation. Make sure that the name is not tricky to spell or pronounce. A complex name will make it more difficult for customers to remember your store. If a customer cannot recall the name or spell it correctly, it makes it challenging for them to recommend the store to other people or look it up in the phone book or on the Internet.

Also, make sure that your store name will not be the same or very similar to another business name. There are various laws that prohibit this from happening, but they are sometimes only enforced if the original owner of the name makes a complaint. Having a name that is the same or similar to another store can sometimes work to your advantage, especially if your store is not as successful as the other store. In this case, potential customers may hear about how great the other store is and want to shop there, but mistakenly go into your store instead. If this happens, you will in effect have gained more customers. However, most new business owners want their store to be the preeminent store in town. They take pride in their venture, so they do not want people mistaking their store for another one. Additionally, they do not want their advertising dollars spent on someone else's business, as customers may mistake the name for that of another store.

See Chapter 7, section **1.2** for more information and examples of business names.

2. Domain Name

You can purchase an Internet domain name for your business. If this name is available at a price you are willing to pay, you should try to buy it as soon as possible. Even if you don't think you want to have an Internet presence right away, you may want it in the future and by that time the name may be taken. You also don't want someone using your name for an online store that sells similar items because it might fool your customers into thinking that they are buying items from your store.

Whether or not you decide to have an online store, an online presence can help you prove that you are a legitimate business.

There are many places online where you can find out if a domain name is available and then register it. Two well-known and largely-used sites are:

- www.smallbusiness.yahoo.com/domains
- www.godaddy.com

3. Fictitious Business Name

If you are not using your legal name in the store's name, such as Jones' Novelties, then you will need to file your "fictitious" name at the local courthouse, county or state office, or government registry. In the United States and Canada, the fictitious business name is also referred to as trade styles, assumed business name, trading as (t/a), or doing business as (DBA).

After you have filed your fictitious business name, you may be required to publish it in your local newspaper for a set period of time. This is done to inform the public of your intent to operate under an assumed name.

In the US, after you have published the statement and there are no claims against it, you will receive an Affidavit of Publication that must then also be filed with the county clerk's office in your area. Check with the Secretary of State or local government registry in the area you will be doing business to determine the requirements for using a fictitious business name.

For corporations in the United States, you must also file a Fictitious Business Name Statement if you are doing business under a name other than the corporate name. Depending on the state in which you are creating your corporation, you may be able to reserve your name on the Internet. This is not a requirement, but if you have a name you would like to use, it is a good idea to reserve it before it is taken.

In Canada, if you are incorporating your business, you will need to do a name search. In some provinces you can go online and do a search through the NUANS system, and in others you will need to complete a Name Reservation or Name Approval Request form through the local government registry.

Filing your fictitious business name may not always ensure that another business cannot use your exact name. The only way to ensure that no one else may use your company name is to trademark or service mark any names, logos, drawings, and the like that you would like to use exclusively to sell your products or services. (See section **10.** for more information about registering a trademark.)

4. Incorporation

Deciding how to structure your business may be an easy or a difficult decision to make. There are plenty of different ways to structure your business and it is worth taking the time to consider the array of various factors and decide which structure is best for you. You will need to ask yourself the following questions:

- Are you willing to give up part of the executive decision-making power?

- Can you find someone that will work as hard and smart as yourself to help run the company?

- Do you want to share the financial risks and rewards with someone else?

- How will your business be taxed?

- Do you want all the ownership and liability with the least hurdles?

- Are you averse to personal liability and risk?

The most common structures a business can take in the United States are: sole proprietorship, partnership, limited liability company (LLC), corporation (C corporation), or S corporation (Inc.). In Canada, you have the option of creating a sole proprietorship or a partnership, or incorporating your business. These structures are outlined in general terms in this section to provide you with a broad concept of your choices. All forms of business are required to obtain a business license and a seller's permit; however, an LLC and a corporation require additional paperwork and fees. To fully understand these business structures, it is a good idea to read specialized books to help you decide which structure is best suited to your business. You should also discuss the options with a professional tax or business lawyer or adviser.

There will be positives and negatives to each of these different types of businesses, and it is not always easy to decide which is best for you and your new company. Keep in mind that the structure you decide to create will affect the amount of work you will need to put into the company, how much profit you can take away from it, and how much you will pay in taxes. It may also affect your relationship with the people you decide to do business with. In general, a sole proprietorship and partnership are the lowest cost and highest risk. Creating an LLC is cheaper than incorporating, but does not offer quite as much protection as a corporation does.

4.1 Sole proprietorship

A sole proprietorship is made up of one business owner called the sole proprietor. This form of business ownership involves the least amount of time, money, and paperwork to set up.

A sole proprietor is completely in charge of his or her own business. He or she has the ability to make all of the decisions for the business and is also responsible for all of these decisions. Therefore, the sole proprietor is the one that benefits from all of the profits the venture makes and is liable for all of the debts that it incurs. The sole proprietor is required to claim all of his or her profits or losses on his or her individual tax returns.

A sole proprietorship is not an incorporated business, but it does have the advantage of low start-up costs. The biggest disadvantage to a sole proprietorship is the unlimited liability, which means you will personally assume all the risks and debts of your company. It can also be difficult to acquire financing.

This type of business is very straightforward to set up. Creating a sole proprietorship in the US requires obtaining a business license and seller's permit (from the State Board of Equalization). It may also require additional licenses or fees from the state and/or city that you will be operating in. Check with City Hall, the State Board of Equalization, or the Department of State for more information about filing your papers and any additional documents and fees. The Internal Revenue Service (IRS) requires that you file the Form 1040 along with Schedule C or C-EZ for your taxes. Schedule C will help you figure your net profit or loss. You will then use this number to complete page 1 of Form 1040. Contact the IRS for more information about business taxes.

In Canada, a sole proprietorship has minimal registration requirements, which include getting a certificate of compliance and a business license, and registrating for a business name and for GST or HST. As a sole proprietor, you will pay taxes by reporting income (or loss) on a personal income tax return (Form T1). The income or loss will be part of your overall income for the year. Your income tax return must include financial statements or one or both of the following forms: Statement of Professional Activities (Form T2032) or Statement of Business Activities (Form T2124). Contact the Canada Revenue Agency for more information about business taxes.

4.2 Partnership

A partnership is similar to a sole proprietorship but requires more than one person to be part of the business. There are two main types of partnerships: a general partnership and a limited partnership.

A general partnership exists when all the partners involved have the same amount of authority to run the business and are all equally responsible for any debts incurred.

A limited partnership is when one or more of the owners have elected not to have equal decision-making authority and everyone in the partnership has agreed to this. Usually, the partner or partners with less authority have less or no responsibility for any debts the business may incur. When a partner has absolutely no authority to make decisions in a limited partnership, the person is commonly referred to as a silent partner. Sometimes a silent partner may not even be known to the public as being a partner in the company.

The biggest advantage of a partnership is the low start-up costs. It is also easy to convert a partnership into a different type of business structure.

The biggest disadvantage is finding a suitable partner or partners to do business with. Taking on a partner adds another level of risk to your venture. When deciding whether or not you want to share the financial risks and the amount of work you will need to do, do not forget the additional risk of the partnership not working out the way you had planned. Even if your business goes well, the partnership may not — there have been many more small-business partnerships that have gone astray than successful ones. In order for your business to run smoothly, you and your partner must be able to work well together or you will be wasting time trying to come to compromises on important business decisions.

In the US, the setup for a partnership is somewhat similar to a sole proprietorship in that it requires obtaining a business license and a seller's permit (from the State Board of Equalization). However, a partnership is required to file Form 1065 called US Partnership Return of Income from the IRS for the business's yearly taxes. The information on this form is given to each partner involved, and they must file an individual Schedule K-1, Form 1065, along with their individual tax forms. Contact the IRS for more information about business taxes.

In Canada, a partnership has minimal registration requirements; these include getting a certificate of compliance and a business license, and registrating for a business name and for GST or HST. As for taxes, the partnership itself does not pay income tax on its operating profits and does not have to file an annual return. Instead, each partner includes a share of the partnership income or loss on a personal, corporate, or trust income tax return. Each partner will need to file financial statements or one or both of the following forms: Statement of Professional Activities (Form T2032) or Statement of Business Activities (Form T2124). Contact the Canada Revenue Agency for more information about business taxes.

4.2a Partnership agreement

If you are considering a partnership, then you should have a legally written partnership agreement. A valid agreement is written with the participation and agreement of all the partners and details how each partner is going to be involved in the business from its inception to its sale or dissolution.

A partnership agreement acts as a guideline on how business between each partner is going to be carried out and enables each partner to understand and have a reference to what his or her role is in the company. A partnership agreement should include clauses for the following issues:

- Participation and/or duties of each partner (i.e., how much money, time, work, and what type of work each partner is responsible for).

- Amount of authority (i.e., how much authority each partner has over the business and the other partners in the business).

- Division of gains and losses (i.e., how the profits and debts will be divided).

- Resolution of disputes.

- Amount of investment from each partner.

- Provisions for death, retirement, or succession.

- Dissolution of the partnership.

- Retaining rights to any business trademarks or patents (i.e., which partner will retain the rights).

Each partner should initial each page of the agreement and sign and date his or her name at the end, agreeing to the statements in the document.

You can create your own partnership agreement by using the assistance of a book specifically designed for this purpose. These books will usually have samples for you to follow. However, it can be easy to miss something you would have liked to include in your agreement. See *Partnership Agreement* from Self-Counsel Press' Forms on CD series for more information.

Hiring a lawyer to help you and your partner create or review a partnership agreement helps prevent you from missing things you might have if you wrote it yourself. A lawyer may also write the agreement in a more clear and concise way than you are be able to.

It is easy to believe that you will never have an argument that cannot be resolved with the person you are creating your business with, but it has happened ever since partnerships came into existence and it continues to happen. There have been many partnerships that have not gone well. Most of the time it is either due to differences in opinion on the way things should be done, or differences in how much work one partner may put in compared to the other partner. Both of these situations can be difficult to handle and having a partnership agreement can explain how you've decided to resolve these situations, should they arise.

However, it is not always obvious at the time what kind of loopholes you may have in your agreement. For example, it may state that each partner must put in as many hours as the other, but it may be hard to quantify depending on the quality of time put into the company. Therefore, one partner might work hard and smart and the other partner might not be doing anything constructive during his or her time spent working on the business.

4.3 US limited liability company (LLC)

In the US, a limited liability company (LLC) is made up of one or more owners. LLCs have limited liability from company debt and can choose between being taxed like a corporation or like a sole proprietorship. This type of company allows small-business owners that don't want to incorporate to have the freedom of limited liability from company debt.

The main advantage of an LLC is that the members are protected from some liability for acts and debts of the company, but are still responsible for any debts beyond the entity's fiscal capacity. In most states, businesses are treated as entities separate from their members. One of the biggest disadvantages of LLCs is that many states levy a franchise tax or capital values tax on them.

To become an LLC you must file Articles of Incorporation with the Department of State in the state in which you will be conducting your business. The filing fee and minimum tax fee vary according to the state.

Another requirement of an LLC is to create an Operating Agreement that details what each partner's participation in the business is going to be. It is not required to file this agreement, but it must be stored in the place of business. Check with your Secretary of State office for any other requirements for LLCs.

4.4 US corporation

A corporation, which is sometimes referred to as a C corporation, is a structure that exists legally as its own entity so that it may continue to run even if one of the owners is no longer with the corporation. Depending on the state in which you will be incorporated, you may or may not need to have more than one person to form a corporation.

The advantage of a corporation is that the owners (called the shareholders or stockholders) are not personally liable for any business debt. They are entitled to enjoy the profits from the corporation without the liability of ever having to owe any personal money as a result of any action of the corporation.

The disadvantage is that running a corporation is more complicated. For starters, since no one is personally liable for any business debts or corporate taxes, the corporation must deal with its own debt. Furthermore, the corporation must file and pay its own taxes. Individual shareholders must also pay taxes on any money they receive as dividends from corporate profits when filing their personal income taxes (even though the corporation has already paid taxes on that money as well). This is referred to by some people as "double taxation." Note that salaries paid out to employees are not taxed on the corporate level and are only taxed as part of personal income.

Dividends are monies paid to shareholders based on the percentage of shares or stocks they own in the company; that is why the owners are called shareholders or stockholders. The corporation can sometimes add more shareholders by selling more stocks and/or bonds to additional people.

The shareholders elect a board of directors to make the executive decisions for the company. To keep the directors from having complete control, corporations require them to have their decisions approved by the shareholders if they are making any major changes (such as selling the business). Having so many people involved in the company definitely makes things more complicated!

Creating a corporation involves filing Articles of Incorporation with the Secretary of State, paying the filing fees, and paying any other fees and/or taxes owed to the Secretary of State in the state in which you are incorporating.

There are several different types of corporations that you may form. Usually there are varying Articles of Incorporation forms that you will need to fill out, such as the Articles of Incorporation for general stock or nonprofit mutual benefit. Check with your Secretary of State to find out more about which options are offered in your state.

4.5 US S corporation

A company must first become a C corporation before it can become an S corporation. After it has incorporated and all of its members agree that it should become an S corporation, the company may file to become one.

There are a few reasons a business may want to become an S corporation. The main reason is for taxation purposes. Shareholders or stockholders of an S corporation can choose to be taxed like a sole proprietorship or a partnership. This allows the company's profits and losses to pass through the company without being taxed before they're received by the shareholders. The shareholders must then pay any tax on the company's profits directly on their individual tax returns.

There are some major restrictions on what types of C corporations are eligible to become an S corporation. You should consult with a business lawyer to learn more about these restrictions.

The steps for creating an S corporation from a C corporation involve filing the IRS Form 2553 (Election by a Small Business Corporation). An S Corporation must file Form 1120S (US Income Tax Return). The IRS advises businesses to wait for the acceptance of Form 2553 before they file Form 1120S.

For more information about S corporations, talk to a business lawyer and a tax adviser.

4.6 Incorporating in Canada

The advantage of incorporating in Canada is that your company will have limited liability, which means you are protected personally from lawsuits and creditors. If the corporation goes bankrupt, your personal property and finances should be safe unless you have provided personal guarantees for the company's debts. This means you will not lose more than your investment. Creditors cannot sue you or your fellow shareholders for debts incurred by the corporation.

The disadvantage to incorporation is the higher start-up costs. With a corporation you will need to deal with shareholders, the board of directors, and officers. There are also more documents that need to be filed, such as Articles of Incorporation, an Annual Return, notices of any changes in the board of directors, and any changes of address of the registered office. The corporation must also maintain certain corporate records, file corporate income tax returns, and register in any province or territory in which it carries on business.

If you are considering incorporating your business, you should contact a business professional or lawyer to help you with the necessary arrangements.

Self-Counsel Press publishes books and kits on incorporation, including the *Incorporation Guide for Canada*.

5. Business License and Seller's Permit

In order for your business to be run legally, you are be required to obtain a business license in your area. In the US, your local city office will have information on how to obtain one. In Canada, local municipal business license offices issue them to business owners.

You will also need to obtain a seller's permit. In the US, you can get one from the State Board of Equalization in the state that you are going to conduct business. In Canada, the provinces and territories differ on their rules about seller's permits. Talk to the clerk at your local municipal government office for more information about obtaining one.

Check with City Hall, the State Board of Equalization, government or city registry, or your Department of State to find out if you need to file any additional documents or pay any additional fees. For example, sometimes there are other business fees such as downtown business or association fees, or county, commercial, or government agency fees.

6. Employer Identification Number or Business Number

In order to pay the IRS or CRA payroll taxes, you will need to get an Employer Identification Number (EIN) in the US, and in Canada, a Business Number (BN). This is

similar to a Social Security (SSN) or Social Insurance Number (SIN) for businesses.

Any business other than a sole proprietorship must get an EIN or BN. As a sole proprietor, you could use your SSN or SIN instead, but it is advisable to get an EIN or BN. However, one of these must be obtained if you are going to hire employees. You must file the applicable forms with the IRS to ontain one. In Canada, you will need to contact the CRA to set up your company's CRA accounts and file a Request for a Business Number.

The EIN or BN assigned to you will be used by the IRS or CRA to keep track of the amount of taxes you pay them. In the US, you may also need to get a state Employer Identification Number from the state in which you are doing business, so that they can also keep track of the amount of state taxes you are paying. The Employment Development Department (EDD) is the office that will issue these numbers. The IRS and the EDD will provide you with all of the information you need to pay your employee federal and state taxes. Check with your local city business office for any additional taxes you may need to pay.

7. Sales Tax and Filing Tax Returns

Each state and province has their own laws and regulations in regards to sales tax. Talk to the IRS or the CRA for more information about business sales taxes and registration in your area. You need to find out what forms you will have to complete and send to the IRS or CRA. If you do not comply fully with your state or provincial sales tax laws, you could end up dealing with fines or levies against your company.

You should ask the IRS or the CRA about filing tax returns. It is better to be knowledgeable of the forms and fees so that you can prepare for your taxes in advance, avoid missing any deadlines, and approximate the taxes owed. To ensure you file your business taxes correctly in the US, get the correct information and forms from the IRS and the State Franchise Tax Board in the state in which you are doing business. In Canada, contact the CRA to find out which forms you will need to submit at tax time.

Tip: If you are going to be submitting the sales tax yourself and you do not yet have an accounting method to keep the sales tax you collect separate from your other income, set up an additional account. This way, you can transfer your sales tax to this account on a regular basis, and when it comes time to pay your sales tax, the money to pay it will conveniently be all in the same place.

8. Business Bank Account

An easy mistake for self-proprietors to make is to neglect to create a separate bank account for a business. This can be a very costly mistake because it can become difficult to distinguish business receipts from personal receipts. It is also easy to look at your personal bank account without recognizing that a portion of it will be used to pay sales tax. Therefore, it is necessary to create a business account separate from personal accounts. The ideal way to handle your finances is to hire an accountant and a bookkeeper from the very beginning.

Doing some research to find out which bank would be the best place in which to set up your business bank account in can save you money and time in the long run. Spending a lot of money on fees and a lot of time in lines at the bank could be money and time better spent dealing with your other business duties.

Banks charge a variety of different fees for a business bank account. Even if it states "free business checking," do not be fooled by the word "free," because there will almost inevitably be fees. For example, my business bank advertises "free checking;" however, they charge fees for deposits made into the checking account as well as for writing checks. Ask to see all of the fees that the bank will be charging your account, in writing.

You may want to inquire whether they have a business line, which is usually a shorter wait than regular lines. It is also important to ask if they keep extra change handy. Some banks have very little change at the teller's disposal. Thus, if you need change and the teller doesn't have any, you may have to wait as they ask all the other tellers if they have coins in their drawers or ask the bank manager to go into the vault, which costs you valuable time.

Tip: Don't forget that the sales tax you are collecting for the government is not part of your income. You must remember to look at your accounting sheets instead of your bank account to figure out how much money you have available. Tax collected will need to be sent to the government either monthly or quarterly, depending on how much income you are making.

Another good reason not to look at the bank account to get an idea of how much profit you have made is that some of this money will be used to replace the goods you sold with new goods, and to pay your other bills.

9. Liability Insurance

Check around with insurance agencies and purchase the best deal you can find on insurance. It is a good idea to buy insurance that covers stolen or damaged merchandise, and that will protect you if someone gets injured in your store.

If your landlord does not have insurance on the building, you may want vandalism or natural disaster (e.g., fire, flood, or hurricane) insurance. If a disaster happens and you cannot operate your business in your location anymore, you will want to make sure that the business survives. The insurance money will give you a financial bridge to pay all of your expenses while you are not receiving any income from the store. It might take months, or even longer, until you can either find a new building in which to locate your business or until the owner of the building rebuilds or restores it. You may also want to purchase insurance that includes relocation costs or other costs which will help your business in case of damage to the store due to natural disasters.

If you hire employees, you will need to make sure that your insurance covers them in case of injury or other incidents. Ask your insurance agent to advise you on all of your insurance options.

10. Trademark or Servicemark Registration

A trademark registers a certain name, logo, or other similar object as something that you can use exclusively on your merchandise to differentiate it from other merchandise. A servicemark is a mark that you exclusively use when advertising the services that you sell.

In the US, you can register a trademark or a servicemark with the Trademark Unit of the Secretary of State in the state in which you will be conducting business. If you would like to use your trademark or servicemark nationally, you should also file it with the United States Patent and Trademark Office.

In Canada, the first step to registering your trademark is to go to the Canadian Intellectual Property Office's (CIPO) online Canadian Trademarks Database to find out if there are any other trademarks that are similar or identical to your own. The next step is to file an application with the CIPO.

6
SETTING UP YOUR RETAIL STORE

The first couple hundred customers that visit your store will quickly spread the news about their shopping experience. You may also have some press coverage when you open, in which the reporter's impressions will be passed on to potential customers. Therefore, you will want to have all of your fixtures and furniture ready to create a nice ambiance right from the start. Your equipment, such as the point of sale system, should be up and running so you have an efficient checkout system. You will also need to have enough products in the store to provide your customers with a good selection. In order to do all of this, you will need plenty of cash and cannot be afraid to spend it!

It is important to have enough start-up capital to get your business off to a good start for several reasons. One reason, is that you will need to purchase everything your store requires to look well stocked and run efficiently. Your potential customers' first impressions are very important to your business.

You may need to do some or all of the following tasks to get your store ready for operation. These tasks can take longer than you imagine because you may run into problems; for instance, you might have electrical wiring problems or the installation person for a service you ordered might have to reschedule the appointment several times. Therefore, make sure that you begin with the tasks you think will take the longest or those that you are unsure about, so that you will have everything completed in time to open your doors to the public.

1. Store Renovations

As soon as you have the keys to your store in hand you can begin to design your store's look. This can be fun and tedious all at the same time!

The first step is to clean the building inside and out. The next is to fix, remodel, or renovate the building on the inside and/or outside to create the store you visualize. You may need to tear down walls and build dressing rooms and a clerk's desk. You might also need to buy or build display racks and wall shelves. You may need to hire a carpenter, call in help from handy friends or family, or if you are handy, you can do it yourself.

Renovations to the inside of the store might include installing a water heater, improving the plumbing, or installing new lighting. Also, you might want to, or be legally obligated to renovate your store to meet the needs of disabled people.

There will probably be electrical work necessary for your store, unless you were lucky enough to move into a place that has all the lights set up the way you want! You may want to install soft lighting for the dressing rooms and bright lights for the adult section. Check for any faulty wiring that needs to be fixed if the building is old or not well maintained.

You should also consider installing security cameras. Video surveillance will help you identify shoplifters, employee fraud or theft, and even burglars. It lets your store employees and customers know that you have the power to see what is going on in the store at all times.

After you have come up with a store logo and a name, you will need to decide on a color scheme for the inside and outside of the store. You may decide to hire a professional painter to do the work or you may want to save money and do the painting yourself. Choose colors that work well with the design and the theme of your store. For example, if you have a store that is small with dark spaces, make sure to choose a lighter color (such as a cream or a very light dusty rose) that will not make the store seem even smaller. If you have decided that the name of your store is "My Lover's Desire" and you choose to use a heart theme, you could pick the dusty rose color for the inside and use a bright red on the outside to draw attention to the store. Color choice is a matter of personal taste. Every good store has its own style, so pick a color that you think fits your business and run with it whether it be fun and flashy, elegant and romantic, alternative or punky, or even futuristic. If you think you can pull it off, go for it!

2. Store Signage

After you have decided on a logo and a name, you will need to create your signage. Will you have a neon sign inside the window, or a big sign attached to the front of the store?

If you decide to hire someone to design, create, and hang your signage, then you may need to order your sign as soon as possible, so it will be ready in time for the store opening. If you are artistic and decide to create your own signage, make sure you leave yourself enough time to complete this task. It may seem simple at first, but it could quickly become overwhelming combined with all the other tasks you need to complete before you open!

Verify with your city, business district, and landlord about any rules, permits, or permissions you may need, especially if you want a big, blinking, or flashing sign. There are different types of sign controls and restrictions that you may need to be aware of.

3. Payment Methods, Equipment, Services, and Supplies

In the midst of your renovations, you will need to decide what equipment and software you'll need for your store. In order to have it delivered to the store in time for opening, you may need to order it sooner rather than later. Some items might end up on back order, so you will need to have a contingency plan should something important be delayed or not available.

3.1 Payment methods

You will need to consider which forms of payment you will accept. There are many choices for payments, including cash, Visa, MasterCard, Discover Card, American Express, checks, and automated teller machine (ATM) cards. All methods of payment have their own advantages and disadvantages, so think critically about which ones you want to accept. I will give a brief description and a few relevant points on each of the most common forms, but keep in mind that details of how different banks and institutions charge and operate are always changing, so you should examine your options.

3.1a Cash

Cash is good! The only risk with cash is theft, so be careful. Empty your register every day and deposit cash in the bank. Be careful when carrying large sums of cash, for your safety as well.

3.1b Checks

Checks are good for vendors because they are a low-cost payment to accept. In general it does not cost anything to deposit one. However, checks have some big risks, so much so that my store stopped accepting them. If a check you deposit bounces, your bank charges you a fee. Many stores try and go after the person who wrote the bad check to recover the money and the fee. Unfortunately, not much usually comes out of this and it can be a lot of work for nothing.

Another problem with checks is that a customer who writes one can call his or her bank and stop the payment. Customers can even do this months after your bank has deposited the money into your account, and your bank might take the money out and issue them a refund. This happened to me once on a fairly large sale. I pursued the matter all the way through to a judgment in small claims court, and the person never showed up or responded to anything. The settlement ended up being several times the original amount, partly because of penalties and partly because of the fees I incurred in prosecuting. In the end the person never paid a dime and completely ignored every communication. I must have spent another couple of hundred dollars paying for court-filing fees, for sheriffs to deliver the court subpoena, and for judgment notices. At one point I even ran a credit check on the person and discovered a history of bad credit and pending bankruptcy. I gave the claim to a collection agency that takes part of the money if it can recover it, and even they gave up after a year. After that I stopped taking checks.

Fortunately, nowadays it seems like everybody with a checking account has an ATM card or a check card with a Visa or MasterCard logo on it. If you take these types of credit cards, you can use this system instead of accepting checks.

Another way to accept checks is to get a check scanning service, in which the routing numbers on the check are used to electronically remove the money from the customer's bank account immediately. This allows you to find out if the check will bounce right before the sale is complete. These systems have significant equipment and transaction fees associated with them.

3.1c Credit cards

This was by far the most common form of payment used in my store. The fees for accepting credit cards are well justified for the convenience and increased buying power they give the customers.

Most credit card processors have nearly identical fee structures for processing Visa and MasterCard and tend to bundle them together. Credit card companies normally charge a small per-transaction flat fee (around $0.20 at the time this book was printed), and a percentage (usually between 1.5 percent and 4 percent).

Rates for Discover Card have become similar to those for Visa and MasterCard. However, the Discover Card is not used nearly as often and you might not want to keep track of additional bills from this type of card.

American Express (Amex) works from a retailer's perspective like a normal credit card; it is just more expensive. Customers like to use their Amex cards because Amex tends to have great rewards programs. The reason Amex can do so is because they charge vendors more than other credit card companies. The percentage of the typical transaction charged by Amex is double those of Visa and MasterCard.

If you do not accept American Express, customers may be disappointed, but they will usually use their Visa or MasterCard as an alternative. From my experience, it seems everyone who has an American Express card has other forms of credit as well.

Credit card readers and modems can be rented or purchased from credit processing vendors. Buying is usually a lower-total-cost way to go than renting, but I would also recommend negotiating with your credit card vendor to see if it might give you one for using its services. If you have a computerized point-of-sale system, a smaller keyboard or a USB card reader can be used, and those are very inexpensive.

3.1d ATM or debit cards

ATM card processing is another popular form of payment. Businesses that profit from accepting ATM cards are ones that do larger transactions.

The disadvantage of accepting ATM cards is that the per-transaction fees a business pays are at the very least twice what credit card charges would be, currently ranging from about $0.40 on the very low end to $2.00. These services also have higher or additional fixed-monthly fees than just accepting credit cards. To compensate for this, many vendors charge the customer an ATM fee to use the feature. Charging a fee to let customers use the debit machine is not always allowable by law, so check it out before you do this.

The advantage of the ATM card is that some companies only charge vendors a flat rate and not a percentage of sales.

To figure out if accepting ATM cards is a cash positive situation for you, look at all of the fees and calculate relative transactions. If you pay a $0.25 per-transaction fee and a 1.5 percent fee for credit cards, and an ATM charge would be a flat fee of $1.00, then the transaction would have to be more than $67.00 for the ATM transaction to be cheaper than a credit card transaction. This does not take into account the additional equipment or monthly service fees. To factor that in, you would have to estimate how many more ATM transactions you would like to do per month and divide the costs per transaction.

To accept ATM transactions you also need to buy a personal identification number (PIN) keypad so that customers can enter their PINs.

3.2 Electronic office equipment

Your point-of-sale (POS) system should include all the forms of payment you will accept at your store. That means if you decide to accept cash, credit cards, and ATM cards, then you will want a system that accepts those forms of payment.

You may decide that you don't want to have a credit card machine, but you will lose sales without one. Some customers wouldn't have the money to pay for items if it wasn't for the availability of credit cards. Sometimes customers even spend more money when they are using a credit card instead of cash. Therefore, the benefits of accepting credit cards will usually outweigh the extra fees you will have to pay.

The next decisions to make are how many POS systems you will need and if you will rent or buy these systems. Renting a machine is costly and you will usually have paid enough money in rent to own the machine within the first two years. Therefore, it is more economical to purchase the machine. You might also be able to find used ones for sale on the Internet or at used office supply stores. The main reason why people rent the machines is because they do not have enough money to purchase one outright.

There are a number of vendors that sell POS systems of various designs and complexities. There are some clear advantages to having your inventory control, credit card processing, transactions, and sales records all connected in one POS system. It gives you instant access to your inventory and sales histories and tax summaries, but the big trade off is in setup and database maintenance time. The more sophisticated systems do, however, have much higher initial costs for the equipment and software.

My store had a fully integrated POS system in which all merchandise was bar coded, and the inventory was tracked item-by-item in the database. This system was almost flawless and ran from a computer that was used for many business functions. It was equipped with a bar code gun, pole screen stand, cash drawer, and receipt printer.

You will also need to purchase a computer, printer, fax machine, photocopier, and telephone for your store. You may need to order specialized software to do your inventory control and accounting.

Don't forget to set up appointments to get your phone and Internet connections! Service people are busy and sometimes it can take a few weeks before they are able to hook up your phone line or Internet.

Having the phone connected and working ahead of time can help you field calls from potential customers who have questions about what you will be selling in your store and when your grand opening will be. It will also be convenient for you to make calls to vendors and other people you will need to call for business or personal reasons.

If you want your business to be listed in the Yellow Pages, tell the telephone company employee at the time you sign up for your phone service, to save time.

3.3 Furniture and fixtures

After you have decided what kind of theme and atmosphere (e.g., Victorian, modern, rock 'n roll) you want to present to your customers, you will need to buy the furniture and fixtures necessary to create this theme.

Research to find fixtures that would display your items most effectively. You may prefer the look of some fixtures over others,

but they might be more expensive. Keep in mind that the extra money you will pay for nicer fixtures for a women- and couple-friendly or higher-end store will usually pay off. If the merchandise looks better on the more expensive fixtures, and the store looks nicer as well, people will tend to purchase more. For example, it has been noted by many fixture professionals that displays that have clothing facing forward are most effective. The clothes are easier to view and do not bunch up like on round racks. Therefore, a lot of large chain stores only have round racks for sale or clearance items so that customers must look through them for deals. Stores that are not secondhand, discount, or other similar type stores do not usually use round racks to display their merchandise.

The following are some of the fixtures you will need to buy:

- Sale racks
- Hangers (make sure the hangers will fit onto the sale racks you buy)
- Slat walls, slat wall hooks, and slat wall shelves
- Grid walls and wire grids
- Sign holders
- Mannequins
- Garment forms
- Sale counters
- Counter top displays
- Jewelry display cases
- Display cases for lotions
- Seasonal decorations for the store

Tip: You may purchase furniture and fixtures new or used. However, often you can purchase new furniture and fixtures at the same or similar prices as used furniture, so comparison shop before you buy. Also, keep in mind the shipping costs for these items.

Vendors can occasionally offer you free fixtures to display their products on, so ask them if they will provide you with any free displays or selling tools.

See the Resource Guide included on the CD for a list of places that sell retail fixtures and supplies.

3.4 Service connections

As mentioned earlier, it is important to order service connections as soon as possible because service people are busy and you may have to wait for an appointment! The following are some of the services you will need to order:

- Utilities (e.g., heat, electricity, water)
- Phone and fax lines
- Internet connection
- Garbage collection
- Cleaning service, if necessary
- Drinking water or bottled water deliveries
- Commercial-free radio service
- Building alarm system (for detecting trespassers and informing you and the police of the intruders).

    If required by your local police or city, you may need to pay fees to have a security system that notifies the police when it goes off.

3.5 Office and cleaning supplies

You will need to purchase office supplies and cleaning equipment. Some of the office supplies you may need to purchase include:

- Clothing steamer
- Price tagging guns
- Pens and pencils
- Computer paper
- Scissors
- Tape (masking and regular tape)
- Stapler
- Hole punch

The cleaning supplies you may need to purchase include:

- Vacuum cleaner
- Cleaning cloths and dusters
- Mops and brooms
- Cleaning solutions (e.g., for floors, counters, and glass displays)

4. Merchandise Packaging

Once you have decided on your store name, whether you will have a logo and/or slogan, and if you will have a website, decide what kind of bags or boxes you will put the merchandise in for customers. At this point you should have decided on a theme and/or color scheme for the store, and you will want to integrate this into your packaging because it is a walking advertisement. The packaging will travel around with the shopper, and if it is unique to your store, people will start to identify it.

You might need to purchase bags, garment boxes, and jewelry boxes. You can choose to have your store information embossed on these items, or you can buy stickers with this information that you can put on the packaging yourself. You may also want to purchase tissue paper to wrap garments in before putting them in gift boxes.

I created a unique logo and designed the color palate and theme of my business around it. Customers started to identify the bags with the store, so when they saw one they thought about coming in to see what new items were in stock.

5. Inventory

Research the type of inventory you would like to carry in your store. Find out what the latest trends are and what is selling.

Take into consideration the demographics of your area when you decide what type of inventory to carry. This demographic make-up will tell you if your customers will have the extra money to pay for higher-end items or if they will most likely be looking for the cheapest items, regardless of the quality.

A great way to figure out what types and brands of items you should carry is to find a lingerie and adult toy trade show to attend. These shows travel to bigger cities in North America, so it may not be feasible to attend one if it is not in your area. If you cannot go to one, you could subscribe to an industry newsletter like *teeze magazine*, which is another way to find out what's current and popular.

You could also do your own research by going into stores that are similar to yours to find out what they are selling. I went to different adult lingerie and toy novelty stores all over California and Nevada right before I started my business to figure out what kinds of items and name brands they carried. I took notes on items I liked, and that is how I came up with the list of merchandise that I needed to order.

After opening my store, I attended multiple trade shows to stay aware of upcoming trends, and I continued to visit stores similar to mine whenever I went on vacation. For example, when I went to Europe I took the opportunity to visit several similar boutiques and was therefore able to identify new brands for my store to carry. Comparing other stores to your own will provide you with a new perspective on how other people design their shops and what they sell.

The first time people come into your store they will want to feel as if they have a lot of different items to choose from, and they will most likely prefer to browse around before they purchase anything. It is important to have more than one of all of your items, but you also want to make sure you don't have too much inventory. When a store has too much inventory it makes it difficult for the customers to browse and they may feel overwhelmed. This is especially true if there are many different styles of clothing, because it makes the store seem like a discount store where a customer has to sift through the merchandise to find something he or she likes.

If your store doesn't have enough inventory, it can create the feeling that your business is about to close down. Also, customers may become frustrated with the lack of styles to choose from, or become upset because you don't have their size in stock. You don't want to run out of products before you can receive a new order, or you might lose the sales you could have made.

6. Wholesalers: Manufacturers and Distributors

Some merchandise can only be purchased from its manufacturer, so you won't be able to choose where you buy it from. However, some wholesalers allow distributors or vendors (whether companies or individual salespeople) to sell their merchandise for them. When you decide to order from wholesalers, make sure to ask them the questions in Worksheet 1 (the worksheet is also included on the CD so you can print it and write down the wholesalers' answers).

The answers to these questions will help you determine the most cost-effective, efficient, and hassle-free way to receive your inventory.

Note that sometimes wholesalers have fixed retail prices, which means they mark prices on their items. This is most common with books and greeting cards. Some wholesalers also require a minimum retail price so their products maintain a good reputation and are not portrayed as cheap in quality due to low retail prices. Furthermore, the wholesaler may not want their customers worrying about having to wage price wars with each other when selling their products. If a wholesaler finds out that one of their customers is not complying with their policies, they can choose not to sell to that customer.

Question 16 on Worksheet 1 discusses hang tags, which are the tags hanging from the clothing that state the price of the product, and more importantly, usually have pictures of models wearing the clothing. These pictures can greatly increase the sales of these items, especially for lingerie that is sometimes difficult to imagine on a person, due to straps, lace, or other tricky pieces that make it hard to display properly.

Ask your wholesaler to recommend how much product you should have per square foot of product space in your store. This figure may vary depending on what type of product it is and what type of display fixtures you have.

You can research vendors on the Internet. The Resource Guide on the CD includes several vendors that you can contact online or by telephone.

7. Setting Prices

Price your inventory to sell, not to collect dust. You need to be realistic when you set prices for your merchandise. If your prices are too high, your customers may feel that they are being taken advantage of; especially if they find out that other places sell the items for a lot less money. Or people coming into your store might not buy anything at all. However, if your prices are too low, you might not be able to cover all of your bills at the end of the month.

Keep in mind that when you sell retail items, you are only making the money that is left after you deduct the total cost of sales. This includes the cost of the goods you sold, the freight and handling charges, and the cost of the packaging that you are using to wrap the goods in after they have

WORKSHEET 1
QUESTIONS TO ASK WHOLESALERS

Company Information

1.   (If ordering from a distributor, ask:) Which manufacturers do you distribute for and which items of theirs do you carry?

2.   How long has your company been in business?

3.   Where are you located?

Order and Merchandise Information

4.   What are your first time, minimum purchase price and piece requirements?

5.   What are your consecutive purchase requirements?

6.   How long will it take you to process my orders?

7.   What terms of payment do you accept?

8.   Do you charge a handling fee?

9.   Will you negotiate prices?

10. Is any of your merchandise on sale?

11. Do you also sell to the general public?

12. Do you have fixed retail prices?

13. Do you have most of your items in stock? (You want to avoid back-order and late-drop shipments as often as possible.)

14. Do you have any kind of guarantee on your merchandise?

15. How is your merchandise packaged?

16. Do you use hang tags?

17. Is your merchandise ready for the customer to use or do I have to tie, lace, or put together anything in order for the item to be worn or used?

Shipping Information

18. What freight carrier do you use?

19. How fast can you send the merchandise to my location?

Return Policy

20. What is your return policy for defective items?

21. If you accept returns, will you give me credit on my next order for the returned item(s) or refund my money?

22. If you give monetary refunds, how long will it take you to refund my money?

21. What is your return policy for items that do not sell in my store?

22. What is your restocking fee for returned items?

been purchased. Freight usually costs between 2 and 15 percent of the cost of the goods. Depending on how fancy you want to get, the average cost of a bag, box, tissue, and other items used to wrap the goods you sell will usually vary between $0.30 and $1.50.

For example, the average wholesale price of a corset is $25. Let's say your wholesaler told you that an approximate shipping charge would be 5 percent of the worth of your merchandise. This would bring your total to $26.25. Now, you will need to divide the $10 handling charge the company added to your purchase by the total number of items you purchased. Let's say you bought 100 items, which would make the handling charge for the corset 10 cents, and brings your total to $26.35. You want your customer to walk away with a nicely packaged product, so you will need to add 20 cents for the bag and 5 cents for the tissue you use. This brings your total to $26.60. You might also want to consider the fact that so many people use credit cards to purchase their items and a typical credit card processor will charge the store 2.5 percent of the gross purchase price (price of the item including taxes) plus $0.20 for the transaction fee. Assume that you price the item at $62.50 and that sales tax in your area is eight percent. Eight percent of $62.50 is $5, so the total is $67.50. If you pay 2.5 percent in credit card fees, that is $1.69, plus the $0.20 transaction fee, which equals $1.89. Add that to the $26.60 and you get $28.49 which is the cost of the sale, $3.49 more than the wholesale price.

This may not seem like a lot of money, but when you add it up for each sale, the total becomes quite large. If you also want to include the cost of salaries and wages you pay your employees, it will bring this total even higher.

The average markup on clothing in adult boutiques is between two to three times the wholesale price. For adult products, this number goes from two and a half all the way up to five times the wholesale price (sometimes even more for adult movies). Clothing tends to have higher wholesale prices and adult products tend to cost less. Usually an item with a high wholesale price will have a lower retail mark-up and an item with a cheaper wholesale price will have a higher markup. Therefore, if you were to mark the corset up to $62.50, the total profit at point of sale would be $34.01. Keep in mind that this profit will be divided into employee wages and other expenses before you take home any of it!

Sometimes your wholesaler will be able to recommend an average markup for their items, or they will actually have a minimum markup for you to use. Another way to research pricing is to check out the competition and see what prices they have set for the items you are selling. The total cost of your sale might be higher or lower than for other stores. Therefore, remember the total cost of the sale when you decide how to price your items. Don't price yourself out of making a profit!

8. Dress Your Window

Window dressing is a very important part of engaging customers on the street to come inside your store and shop. There are books dedicated to window dressing that may be very helpful to you, but here are a few tips to keep in mind:

- Do not place anything in the window that you do not sell, besides necessary items that you are using to display the merchandise.

- Use bright lights and display merchandise with bright colors, so people passing by will notice it and be able to see the merchandise clearly.

- Have your lingerie on mannequins so that people can see what the clothes will actually look like on a body.

- Make sure that clothes are steamed and not wrinkled.

- Use several height and width levels to make it more interesting to look at. You can use boxes, stools, and chairs, or place items toward the front and toward the back of the display.

- Shapes and colors can be repeated to create fluidity and make it more pleasant to look at.

- Do not display so many things that it looks cluttered.

- Keep it clean.

- You may want to use something that moves or flickers, because eyes are drawn to motion.

- Make sure it portrays the character of your store and that anyone seeing it would get an idea of the type of merchandise you carry.

There may be restrictions in your area for what you can place in your window display, ranging from what types of lights to what types of items. Check with your city code if you are planning on having a very flashy or provocative window display.

9. In-Store Merchandise Displays

In-store merchandise displays are used to show off the product in the most ideal way possible in order to entice the customer into purchasing it. These displays can include mannequins, jewelry showcases, Styrofoam heads, or jars and vases, and can be assembled in any creative ways you can think of. The following are some suggestions on what products will look best in these displays.

Mannequins make fabulous merchandise displays because people can see what the clothing will look like when worn. Therefore, the more mannequins you can use without making the store look overcrowded, the better. Mannequins are sold in different sizes, shapes, colors, materials, and parts. For example, some come in torsos only and some are only the front half of a torso. The half-torso mannequins are designed to be hung against a flat backdrop. Some stores hang these on the walls, from the ceiling, or in front of the lingerie they have out on the floor.

Mannequins also vary hugely in price. Choose one that suits your purse, and that is the best fit for the place you are going to put it and the mechandise you are planning to display on it. For example, if a mannequin comes with a head, it will make a great display for hats, wigs, tiaras, and sunglasses. If it comes with legs and feet, it will make a great displays for hosiery, shoes, and ankle bracelets. If it comes with arms and hands, it will be even more versatile because not only can you use it to show off bracelets, rings, gloves, and other items, but you can also place merchandise such as ostrich tickle feathers or whips in its hands!

Put merchandise on the fixtures and furniture in places where they are not in the way of the customers, but are still noticeable. For example, you can place boas on top of the clothing rack bars.

Purchasing a lot of merchandise displays can get pricey. Therefore, be imaginative with the ones that you buy so you can get away with purchasing less of them.

Use jewelry showcases and displays to highlight the merchandise's brilliancy. Make sure you do not clutter the display case. Countertop displays are good for displaying several types of items, such as products that you want to stand out, merchandise that is difficult to display elsewhere, or items that can be impulse buys. For example, you could display tiaras, satin gloves, toe rings, or mini whips on counter displays.

Tip: Do not forget to purchase a countertop display mirror if you are selling jewelry. Customers shopping for jewelry usually want to see how it looks on them before they make a purchase.

Styrofoam heads are handy for displaying wigs and tiaras. Jars and vases can help display tall items, such as various types of feather ticklers, fake red roses, candy lollipops shaped like different anatomical parts, and riding crops. The riding crops I display in my store are very popular with younger couples, because the end of the crop is shaped like a red heart and they look cute.

Have in-store testers so customers will be tempted to buy a product if they like it. Often, customers will proactively try these items on by themselves, but if not, they also make great conversation starters and sales tools for your staff.

Another way to encourage sales is to put a few items near the cash register for last minute add-ons. These items are usually cheap accessories or novelties so the customer does not have to think too hard about buying them; for example, small packets of lube or small games for couples (such as love dice or coupons for lovers).

Also, don't forget to ask your wholesalers if they have in-store displays for their merchandise that you can have. Wholesalers will often provide you with the merchandise displays designed for their products for free. They like this because it gives their brands higher visibility.

A well-merchandised store will make the displays a seamless part of the store. The displays will show off the merchandise instead of standing out among the merchandise. Coordinate the placement of your displays so that they don't stand out from the rest of the furniture and fixtures either. Use the merchandise displays you purchase, along with your creativity, to come up with ways of displaying the merchandise that make the items look their best and make it easier for the customer to envision using or wearing the products.

Tip: Decorate your store during the holidays, but make sure that it does not overshadow the merchandise you are trying to sell. Decorations are meant to add festivity to the atmosphere and remind people that shopping for whichever holiday it is should be fun and exciting. Just be careful not to use so many decorations that the products are hard to spot.

7
Marketing and Advertising Your Business

Creating an effective marketing plan is essential to generating more business for your store. Building a strong and loyal customer base takes time and money. You will need to develop a marketing strategy that creates positive brand recognition among the community in which you want most of your customers to come from.

Neglecting to advertise has often been the downfall of many small businesses. Frequently, new business owners will begin to worry about the flow of money from their bank accounts and think that they should try to save money by not advertising. However, the only thing that happens when you don't spend money on effective advertising, is that new customers and returning customers are not prompted to shop at your store. Advertising doesn't have to be expensive, but it does have to be done in order to remind current customers to keep shopping at your store and to bring in new customers. Everybody is aware that Coca-Cola sells soda, but they still keep advertising heavily. They do so because it works and it is necessary.

1. Marketing Your Business

A strategic marketing plan is essential to attracting new customers to your store and maintaining current customers, while at the same time making sure that you are not wasting your money on ineffective advertising. This plan is meant to help you establish your business's reputation. While your business plan is meant to guide how you run the company and touches on your marketing strategy, your marketing plan provides the details of how you will carry out this strategy. Therefore, without a marketing plan, the exact details of how of the company will accomplish and manage its marketing is sometimes lacking.

Having a well-thought-out marketing plan versus a haphazard one could mean the difference between having a profitable business and an unprofitable one. Not all stores develop an entire marketing plan, but those that do tend to be more profitable. Small business owners tend to create business plans rather than marketing plans because investors want to see their business plans but not always their marketing plans. Your marketing plan should be designed for you to use as a resource that will help you carry out the marketing strategies you outlined in your business plan. It may include a mission statement, a brand, a name, a logo, an advertising plan, and a business development plan. The elements of a good marketing plan are explained in the following sections.

1.1 Marketing plan mission statement

The first step to creating your marketing plan is to develop a character for your store, which is done by creating a mission statement and branding your business around its concept. A mission statement is a short statement that is usually written at the top of company reports and states what the company is in business to do. It should be short and to the point so you can tell it to someone in less than ten seconds. The following statement is an example:

To create a happy and healthy environment for adults to shop for quality adult toys and lingerie.

A marketing plan mission statement is often referred to as the company's motto because it sums up what the company was created for and what its unique position is within the market place.

1.2 Store name

The store name should be something memorable that people can pronounce. Remembering the name of your store is important for people trying to locate it in the phone book or on the Internet. It is also important that people can figure out what you sell by your store name. For example, "Spice of Life" may sound catchy and memorable, but people may mistake it for a store that sells spices. Something catchy and memorable could be "Pleasures of the Heart" or "Secret Desires." These are names that would help people pronounce, remember, and identify what you sell.

1.3 Logo

After you have decided on your store's name you can start designing a unique logo that suits it. A simple logo with a minimal amount of colors will help people recognize it faster and will keep printing costs down. For example, if you choose the name "Secret Desires," you could create a logo that looks like pouting lips with a forefinger or a feather crossing vertically over the lips as if making a gesture to be quiet.

When I created and trademarked the logo for my business name, "Naughty Or Nice," it was one red heart with purple horns, overlapping a white heart with a yellow halo. Customers thought it was cute and sexy and would ask to have some of my stickers to put on their cars or other places, which was great as it advertised my business for free! Also, having a logo people think is cool tends to grab their attention when they see it in advertising.

Many companies simply make their business brand name into their logo by making it unique; for example, eBay and Trader Joe's. The fonts these companies chose to use for their brands are youthful and cheery, and are meant to signify their images. You could also make your logo out of your company name. For example, if you wanted to use the name "Private Pleasures" for your business, you could use a thick and cursive font to signify sophistication, or a bold and modern font to signify youthfulness and assertiveness.

The colors in your brand name and logo are also very important, as they are often associated with certain feelings. When people see a logo, and therefore, its colors, they may identify the company with the feelings they already associate with these colors. Many companies, such as Trader Joe's, Costco, and Exxon, probably use red because it is more noticeable in a sea of other colors and is associated with excitement (and sometimes, a good bargain). Other companies, such as Wal-Mart and Chevron, most likely use the color blue in their brand names because they want people to associate them with peacefulness, trustworthiness, and loyalty. White is also used by some companies, such as Aquafina, because it is associated with cleanliness. The color you choose for your unique brand will depend on what feelings you want your customers to associate with it. If you are stuck, there are many companies devoted to selling services that help companies decide on colors to use in their logos.

If you want your customers to associate a multitude of emotions with your company name, you may want to use several colors in your logo or brand name. While companies such as Pepsi and BMW may have only one or two colors in their brand name, they use several more colors in their logos. Each color signifies an emotion they want their customers to identify with their products. Therefore, as an example, if you choose to use the name "Private Pleasures" for your store, you could use bright red for the lips with a black forefinger or a deep purple feather. The color red is associated with excitement, the color black with sophistication and desire, and the color purple with royalty and premium.

1.4 Store brand

Branding your store should make customers identify it as the place to purchase whatever it is that you have identified in your mission statement. Your brand should represent you as being the expert or having the best merchandise for your customers' needs. A brand identity includes your company name and possibly a logo, a slogan, a catch phrase, a theme (e.g., modern or Victorian style), or other things that will make your customers think of your store.

A slogan or catch phrase can help customers remember your store name if you do a lot of television or radio advertising. A catch phrase is usually short, catchy, and direct. Having a theme for your store will help you create ambiance. For example, some lingerie and adult boutiques use the Victorian, modern, or racy decorative style accompanied with classical or modern music to get their customers in the mood for extra shopping.

1.5 Business cards

Well-designed business cards provide a practical and professional way to give your contact information to customers, vendors, or other people you'd like to make aware of your store. They are also a great way of marketing your business. Have a stack of them handy in your store for customers to take as they want. Often, if customers like your store a lot, they will take several cards to give as referrals to other people they know.

A good way to use these business cards as a marketing tool is to keep them handy with you wherever you go and to pass them out whenever a good opportunity presents itself. For example, you can hand them out whenever you talk to someone about your store, or when you notice someone wearing a particular brand of product that you sell. You can also leave them in places, like nearby clubs or bars, as mini-advertisements.

Items that are important in the design of a business card include:

- The name of the business.
- Your business logo. (If you do not have a logo, use a picture of the store or of a product you sell, or another picture that make your business card interesting and will catch the eye of anyone looking through a stack of cards.)
- The name of the business owner(s).

- The business address, telephone and fax number, and website address.
- Days and hours of operation.
- What you sell.

2. Advertise

Advertising lets people know that you are in business, what you sell, where you are located, and anything else you would like the receiver of the advertisement to know. Therefore, it is something people generally acknowledge as important for businesses to do. Advertising can be expensive, so some business owners decide not to do it. However, the cost of effective advertising is outweighed by the cost of lost opportunities to gain customers if you don't advertise. You will not gain customers if they do not know you exist, or if they don't think of your store as the first place to go to buy what they need. Advertising can do both: educate potential customers of your existence and lead them to think of your store first when they want to purchase something that you carry.

A complete retail sales strategy starts when you give your potential customer the idea to come into your store and ends when he or she has made a purchase at your store. Therefore, if you want to succeed, you have to be proactive about getting customers to come into your business. This means you have to advertise in the right places and make more money with the advertising than you spend on it.

Traditional advertising ideas are easy to come up with — newspapers, magazines, direct mailers (e.g., postcards), door hangers, radio ads, and the Yellow Pages — and are all potential ways to advertise. If done correctly, these methods can bring in a lot of business for small retailers; however, these are expensive ways of advertising. The following sections discuss some less expensive ways of advertising your business.

2.1 Before you open ... advertise!

A very important part of advertising your store happens before you even open it, if you are savvy enough to advertise correctly. All too often a business owner will be working on his or her new store for months before the doors open, and there will be no (or very little) information about the store being circulated to the general public. Getting information out about your store will allow you to build up a customer base before you even open your doors. To generate interest before you even open, you could place huge posters in all of your store's windows advertising your opening date; pass out flyers in front of your store; ask the newspaper to run a feature article on your upcoming business; participate in community events; and do any other types of advertising that you think would generate public interest in your store. This way, when you open your doors, there will already be customers ready to shop!

You could also ask other local business owners if they would mind putting up flyers advertising your new store in their windows, and you could start developing business relationships with them so that they will be excited about your store and tell their own customers that it will be opening soon. Word of mouth can be one of the best forms of advertising.

2.2 Advertising through the community and charity events

Get involved with your local business community by introducing yourself and your new venture to local business owners and associations, or the Better Business Bureau (BBB). Being involved in a community of local business owners is a great way to create more business for everyone. When you have good relationships with the other business owners you can co-advertise with them, refer good places to advertise to each other, refer customers to each other's stores, and get neighborly help when you need it.

A good business development plan should enhance your volume of customers by making people want to shop at your store due to the positive feelings they associate with it. Part of this plan should be to invlove your business with the local community so that its members will appreciate your store for its contributions, and feel that you are a permanent part of their community.

Becoming involved with the community is a way to make local customers feel that they are in turn supporting their community by shopping at your store. At the same time, it is a good form of advertising because it helps spread the news that you are in town. A lot of the time, charities and other good-will organizations will have raffles or auctions in which people can bid on items that local businesses have donated. In these instances you can donate an item from your store, like a gift certificate or money. You can also participate in the community by sponsoring an event, which usually gets your name on a handout that is given to the participants of the event.

Another way to get involved in the community is to advertise with other local businesses. This shows comradeship and that you are clearly accepted by the other businesses.

2.3 Trade shows

Participating in retail trade shows is a great way to attain more customers and network with other companies that you could form business development relationships with. Usually people attending trade shows are interested in buying goods and services in the near future, so these people are great prospects for customers. For example, you may want to have a booth at a bridal or lingerie show.

Do not get industry or wholesaler trade shows and retail trade shows confused. The former is for wholesalers (manufacturers and distributors) to sell their merchandise to retail stores and the latter is for retail shops to sell their products to the general public.

If you have never been a vendor at a trade show, it would be a good idea to take a day class at a local community college to learn how to set up a booth and interact with customers. Other ways to learn about being a vendor at a trade show include referring to a book on the subject; attending a trade show and observing (or asking the vendors that you think are doing a good job of attracting people to their booth how they do it); doing an Internet search for tips; or speaking with organizers of shows to find out if they have any suggestions on where to find more information. Since trade shows can be such great opportunities to create partnerships and gain customers, it would be well worth spending extra time and money on learning how to effectively participate in them.

There are many resources for locating trade shows. You can look on the Internet or in newspapers and trade magazines, or you can ask other business colleagues if they know of any upcoming shows. Remember to consider sex toy conventions in large cities, and other events that you could use to showcase your store. Sometimes you'll be able to find events such as "black and blue balls" and "erotic exotic balls."

Tip: Sometimes thinking outside of the box can help you come up with great ways to market your store at trade shows. For example, I attended bridal shows for my business and I was the only vendor there that catered to brides' intimate apparel, wedding night, honeymoon, and bachelorette party needs.

2.4 Client referrals and development

Attracting customers that are shopping at different stores plays a role in business development. Usually, the owners at other stores will agree to refer clients to your store as long as you are willing to refer clients to their stores. A few of the stores that an adult boutique can create mutually beneficial business relations with are bridal stores, bakeries, and photography studios.

Bridal stores are great to have a connection with because the brides shopping at these places will also want to shop for undergarments for their wedding, lingerie for their wedding night or honeymoon, bachelorette party supplies, and bridal shower gifts. Customers shopping for these types of items at your store usually need a wedding dress or know a person that needs one.

Bakeries are great because you can refer clients to them for bachelor, bachelorette, or bridal shower cakes, and they can refer your store for the party supplies and gifts.

Photography shops that do boudoir pictures are also good for giving referrals to buy lingerie at your store. Plenty of people ask where they can get boudoir photographs taken so you could recommend the photography store in return.

There are a lot of different possibilities for creating new business development. For example, you could offer discounts to dancing groups such as ballet, belly dancing, and stripper groups; or groups such as fetish and biker clubs. You could also create your own frequent shoppers' club to give customers an incentive to purchase more frequently at your store.

Creating positive public relations with other businesses and within the community will help your store build good will. By joining your local Chamber of Commerce, Business Development Organization, or other similar organizations, it will provide you with the opportunity to participate in the making of the local business environment. This help you to ensure that the laws and policies of your city allow you to keep your business running efficiently.

2.5 Create a website

A powerful and less expensive advertising medium is the Internet, which can be an especially powerful tool for adult boutiques.

Adult boutiques benefit greatly from having professional websites. Customers may find a store's website through an Internet search engine such as Google or Yahoo!, or might go directly to it if they have the website's address. Printing your store's website address on other forms of advertising provides customers with a way to pre-shop at your store. Many people looking at an advertisement for an adult boutique would like to shop at the store, but are afraid of what the experience would be like. Therefore, having a website where people can see pictures of the store, read about what it is like, and see some of the products it sells will put potential customers at ease with a good first impression of what your store offers.

A website is a great selling tool as well. Internet-only stores have the advantage of having no overhead and therefore do not have to recover overhead costs before they make a profit.

If you decide to also have an online store, making it stand out among the competition is entirely possible. First of all, customers may see your ads and patronize your business, but perhaps they do not want to shop in a retail store. If this is the case, they have the option of shopping at your online store. Second, repeat customers may want to continue to shop at your store, even if they do not have time to come into your store or if they move. Third, customers may prefer the look of your online store, the refund or shipping policies, or some other special features.

Having a professionally-run website is just as important as having a professional-looking store. A website is a reflection of your business and will make an impression on the viewer. Your store could be the most beautiful and organized store in the world, but if customers are looking at your website and it is not up to professional standards, their impression of your business will be poor and they may not want to shop in your store because they may expect it to resemble the website. You would not expect a customer to prefer to shop in an unorganized store if he or she had a lot of choices (and on the Internet, the customer does have a lot of choices), don't expect the customer to want to shop on a messy website either. Your website should look neat, be organized, be easy to use, and have all of the information and functions that shoppers expect.

If you do not know how to create a website, hire a professional to do it for you. It takes a lot of knowledge to create a professional-looking website and it will probably take you a very long time to create one on your own. The sooner you have a good website the better. Customers almost don't believe your store exists if they cannot find information about your store on the Internet! Although my store received almost all of its profits from people shopping in the actual brick-and-mortar store, more than half of my customers told me that they came because I had a nice website.

Internet sites need to be constantly updated with new merchandise (and any old or sold-out merchandise should be removed from the site), and other information that might change needs to be up-to-date. This all takes a lot of time. You will have to update much of this information on a daily basis, and also process any orders. Try to be realistic as to whether you will have time to run the site yourself. If you do have the time, consider hiring someone to show you how to run the site (most likely the person that created it). If you don't have time, you can hire a professional to do the work for you, or you can assign this task to an employee.

Eventually, my store was getting half of its business from its Internet site, about a quarter of its business from walk-by or drive-by traffic, and another quarter from other advertisements I had placed. Many people found the online store by doing an Internet search for the products the store sold, or they would see an ad with the website address and then visit the site to see what the store was like before coming in. Some customers purchased items from my online store; however, many of them used the online store to decide what they wanted to purchase and then would come into the retail store to do so. These types of customers are sometimes too embarrassed to browse in a retail store where people might see them and also don't want a package delivered to their door, or they simply may not have the time to browse in the retail store when it is open for business.

Tip: Salespeople selling advertising on Internet directories often mislead business owners into thinking that a business must advertise in their directory. You need to figure out whether it is worth the money, especially as the number of directories increases from year to year. Ask yourself if there are other businesses listed under your heading that you would be competing with and whether the usage of the specific directory (not the distribution) is measurably significant. If you are within the demographic group that you want your customers to be in, a good rule of thumb is that if you use a particular directory or other advertising media more than others, chances are other people do as well.

3. Place Your Advertising

Placing advertising for your business may sound like an easy task, but it is one that many business owners procrastinate on for a variety of reasons, such as not wanting to spend the money or thinking that their customers will eventually stumble through the front door. Many businesses fail because they refuse to follow good business rules and buy effective advertising. Advertising lets people know that you are in business and why you are better than your competitors so that you will gain customers.

After you have done a thorough investigation of the most effective places to advertise and found some that are within your budget, contact the salesperson at the company you want to buy the advertisement from. Do not buy the advertisement before you have tried to negotiate price, size, position, color, frequency, or any other factors that may affect bang for your buck. Almost all advertising agencies will most likely negotiate heavily with you, especially as their publication deadline approaches.

As mentioned in section **2.**, keep in mind any advertising that you can get for free or can do for yourself at a very low cost. For example, you can create a customer mailer and send out monthly advertisements to the people on your list, you can get newspapers to write up a story on your business, you can pass out flyers (you may need a permit in some areas), you can have your vehicle decorated with advertisements, or you could give small items to an auction or to events in which they will state that the item was donated by your store.

After figuring out where your advertisements would be most effectively placed, the second most important thing is the actual copy of the ad. Often, business owners do not spend enough time on the ad copy, especially when the agency tells them that it can create an advertisement for them. However, just as you do not want your ad placed on a billboard hidden behind a building or in a newspaper none of your customers would read, you do not want an ad in a great spot, that nobody will notice because it blends into all the other advertisements since there is nothing to distinguish it from the other ads. You also don't want people to mistake your advertisement for someone else's because you didn't notice that the name of your company was left out of it. When you are creating your advertisement, remember to include the following information so it will be difficult for potential customers to miss it:

- Business information (e.g., the business name, address, telephone number, directions, and website URL).

- Logos and/or slogans your business may have.

- Information about what you sell.

- Why your services and/or products are the best (if you have competitors).

- Make an offer such as a free gift, a discount, a buy one get one free, or something else that grabs the reader's attention.

- Include a call to action for the readers so that they will want to act on your offer right away. For example, place an expiration date on the discount or state that the sale will continue until the product sells out, and that supplies are limited.

- Put in a picture that may catch someone's attention and that relates to what your business sells.

- Make the shape of the advertisement different than other people's advertisements.

- Use color to make the picture stand out.

Try not to clutter your advertisement with too much text or color, or your reader may not bother trying to read it. Make sure that there is still enough whitespace in your advertisement that the reader does not feel overwhelmed with too much information.

Never forget that you are advertising your business to make customers come into your store and spend money so you will make a profit. There are four major ways that some businesses lose money through advertising:

- The ad is in the wrong location, where nobody notices it, like on a billboard behind a tree or in a part of the newspaper nobody reads (even if it is a popular newspaper).

- The ad is too small for anyone to notice, or it is too large. (An ad is too large if the reader would have noticed it if it were smaller. This may not be a problem for companies with a lot of money to spend on advertising, but when you have a limited budget, you may be giving up your monetary ability to advertise in other places because of the extra money you spent on the larger ad.)

- The ad has coupons or promotions that make it so you are unable to cover your costs. Promoting sales or loss leaders (items sold below wholesale cost) can sometimes be just as bad for business as not getting those customers to come into your store in the first place (even though you are bringing in new customers). While some large chain stores promote loss leaders, most small retailers cannot afford to do this. You might gain customers from selling loss leaders, but you will need to have enough money to pay for these items and also pay your bills.

Although advertising salespeople can sometimes be difficult to deal with, as they will always want you to spend more money, keep in mind that you are advertising for the benefit of your store and not for the salespeople. One of the first things a salesperson is taught is to control the buyer through asking him or her key questions and giving the buyer suggestions that are meant to influence his or her decision to spend more money on advertisements. Do not be intimidated by salespeople and do not let them control the time of the meeting, place of the meeting, or the way the conversation carries on. Remember that you want the best bang for your advertising buck, not for their commission.

4. Include a Call to Action

Sometimes people may see your advertisement and not react to it right away, because there is no call to action. A call to action is a phrase that tells the customers that they should come into the store. This could be because they need to purchase something for a special occasion (such as Valentine's Day), or because there is a sale that they must not miss out on. Advertised, time-limited sales are always a great way to get customers to respond to the advertisement by coming into the store or buying more merchandise while they are in the store.

A few examples of commonly advertised sales are percentages or dollar amounts off, "buy one get one free," and "X amount of money off if the customer spends Y amount." If you are ever at a loss for a new advertising idea, simply look at current advertisements on the television or in the newspaper for ideas from other retail stores. Sales are used by most retail stores large and small. Significant retail sales are usually held in January, to spur more buyers because the season is slow, and also during August and September.

5. Track Your Advertising

After your advertisements have been distributed, create a spreadsheet that will track where your customers heard about your store. This spreadsheet should include all of the places you have advertised. When you ring up a sale, ask the customer where he or she heard about your store and then place a check mark next to the corresponding ad so that you know where people are actually finding out about it. Keeping track of this will enable you to find out which ads were the most effective, so that the next time you need to renew one, you will know if it is worthwhile.

Figuring out which ads are bringing in the most customers will help you decide which to renew and which to concentrate more of your advertising budget on. It is great when customers actually bring in your advertisements or tell you on their own where they heard about your store, but most of the time they will either forget to bring in the coupons or they will not mention where they heard about your store unless you ask them. Therefore, you need to be diligent about asking customers.

After you determine how most of your customers are hearing about your business you can then calculate which advertising was worth your money. For example, if an ad cost $300, you will want to figure out how much money it brought in. If customers spent $600 as a result of an advertisement, then you can figure that about $240 of that was on clothing and packaging that you will have to replace. Out of the $360 left, $300 went to paying for the ad. This means that you made $60 from the advertising. However, you will hopefully have gained new, repeat customers as well. Of course, the more bang for your buck the better, so it is important to figure out which advertisements gave you the best overall return on your investment.

8
STORE POLICIES

Creating store policies before your store opens is important because it will keep you from being put on the spot when you do open and a customer asks you about them. Creating store policies and stating them in an obvious place will inform everyone of your store's rules. By doing so, your customers and employees will most likely not try to violate these rules. Of course, no matter what you do, a few people will choose to ignore your policies. This chapter includes a few key store policies that you may want to create.

1. No Photos

A hurdle in keeping the store pleasant for everyone's shopping pleasure is when people come into the store and play dress up by trying on outfits and taking pictures of themselves. Not only does this distract you from your customers, but it may ruin the clothing. Also, taking pictures in an adult store invades other customers' privacy. Customers are entitled to their privacy and that means a "no photos" policy is a must.

The following is an example of why one customer became annoyed while shopping in my store. The customer was a middle-aged woman that had come out of the dressing room to ask her friend if the intimate outfit she was wearing looked good enough for her 25th wedding anniversary. At the same time, a girl took a picture of her friend coming out of the dressing room in her outfit, and caught the middle-aged woman in the photo too. The middle-aged woman was quite upset at being potentially photographed in intimate apparel. I asked the girl to delete the picture from her digital camera and told her that either I needed to hold the camera at the front desk or she needed to leave the store. Like most people, she was not trying to cause other customers harm or embarrassment, so she deleted the picture and let me hold her camera until she was done shopping. This happened despite a "no photos" policy in the store. Therefore, if you see a person with a camera, ask the person to leave it at the cashier's desk while he or she is in the store.

I had several signs in my store that stated "No Photo Taking Allowed." One was located near the entrance of the store, there was one on each of the dressing room doors, and there was another by the door that led to the 18-and-older adult toy, novelty, and DVD section. I noticed that not everyone read these signs, and that very few people bothered to read signs that were longer than four words or that were in small type. So, if you decide to have signs in your store, make sure to keep the wording as brief as possible and the font large enough that people will read them automatically when they see them.

2. Returns

Since your store will most likely not allow any returns on adult toys, you will have a lot of angry customers if they purchase adult toys that do not work properly and cannot return them. I have heard many times from customers that other stores did not battery test the adult toys, and as a result they were stuck with toys that did not work. By battery testing the toys in front of the customers before they leave the store, they feel better about the no-return policy and know that you sold them a working product.

Some customers will try to return items even after they have used them and even if it has been months (sometimes years) since the item was purchased. One time a man came into my store hoping to return an adult toy he had purchased three months before. He explained that the toy had been his wife's favorite, but because it broke, he wanted a refund. However, with used adult toys, it is a hygiene issue to handle them or to try and investigate why they broke; therefore, it is best to not look at, handle, or accept returns on these items. If returns on adult toys are accepted, it can turn into a financial strain. The items will have to be thrown away because they cannot be resold.

You should never resell adult items that have been returned because there is no guarantee that the customer did not use the adult toy. Also, you probably do not want to see a used adult toy in your store!

I have also seen plenty of customers try to return clothing or wearable toys they said they never wore, when it is obvious they have worn the items because of stains. It is also very common for customers to try to return costumes, wigs, and jewelry because they already wore them to the event for which they bought them.

Irrational customers may threaten to report your store for not accepting their returns, but keep in mind that there is no law that states that you must accept returns. The easiest way to handle irate customers that are trying to return used merchandise that you do not feel comfortable accepting, is to create a store policy regarding returns. Print the policy on every receipt, place a sign stating this policy somewhere near your register, and stick to the policy when one of these customers decides to give you a hard time about it. There will always be difficult customers to deal with, but trying to mitigate how much trouble they can cause while in your store is a good idea so that your other customers will not be distracted by them. Although customers may believe it is a right to return or exchange items, it is only a convenience and privilege that some stores offer.

3. Age Restrictions

You may be required to have a legal age restriction inside your store because of the items you sell, or you may only feel comfortable allowing people aged 18-and-up in if you sell adult items.

Some adult stores allow people under 18 to enter and shop in their stores if they also sell items that aren't classified as "adult" products. These minors are restricted from shopping in the areas the adult products are located. In this case, there are usually signs posted in front of the room or dividing structure that sells adult products. If the store only sells restricted products or has no dividing room or structure between these and other products, there will usually be a sign on the entrance of the business stating that only people aged 18 and older are allowed to enter. It is not legal to allow people younger than the age of 18 to view any pornographic material, so you need to be diligent about enforcing the necessary age restrictions.

Many stores have signs that simply say "18 and older only," and other businesses use more words on their signs such as "No minors allowed in the store. You must be at least 18 years old to enter. If you look younger than the age of 25, your ID will be checked by our staff." The amount of words on the sign is not very important, unless you are required by law to include specific statements. Most people identify the number 18 with having to be that age to enter, so they usually don't need to read the whole sign. Just like in liquor stores and grocery stores, when people are purchasing alcohol or tobacco, some stores have stricter policies on checking ID. Some check almost everyone, while others check people only if they do not look of age.

Check with your city to find out if there are specific laws on what signage your store is required to post, where you need to place these signs, and how you are required to enforce laws.

4. Group Restrictions

If you have a lot of young people (by young I mean 16-21 years old) that come into your store at once, you may restrict them to groups of three at a time. This makes it easier for you to watch them to make sure they do not cause any mischief.

Tip: You might not want groups of young people in your store at all because they tend to not purchase anything, except at Halloween if you sell costumes. If you do want their business during Halloween (and this could be a substantially large amount of your sales) you should still be cordial to them throughout the year, as reputations spread and you do not want them boycotting your store.

Depending on how often you expect these groups to come into your store, you may or may not want to post a sign on the front of your store entrance. A lot of signs or wordy signs at the front entrance tend to detract from the look of your store, and people will not bother reading multiple signs anyway. Therefore, only place the most important information on any signs you post. Since I did not want a lot of younger groups of customers coming in the store all at the same time, I posted a sign on the wall behind the cash register in small print in regards to group restrictions. When I asked people to leave the store, I would point out the sign. This way they did not feel like I was picking on them, but that the sign had the authority.

5. Employee or Merchandise Abuse

If a person is disruptive, or verbally or physically abusive to you, your employees, or other customers, you do not have to put up with it. Throw the abuser out! Your paying customers should not be distracted from their shopping by rude people. If someone is being disruptive or misbehaving, simply ask the person to leave. If a person refuses to leave, calmly tell them you will call the police if he or she does not leave. If the person refuses again, call the police immediately. Do not try and escalate any situation with a customer and do not touch them. If you physically throw someone out of your store, you could likely expect a lawsuit.

There is no need to post a sign stating a behavioral policy, as good behavior on private property is implied and does not need to be stated.

6. Dressing Rooms

State how many people are allowed in a dressing room at one time — preferably only one person. You will also need to be clear on how many items are allowed in. Your policy should explain whether the customers are allowed to take merchandise in and out on their own or if they are to leave the merchandise in the dressing room after they have tried it on (if they do not want to purchase the items).

Also state your try-on policies. For example, if you allow panties to be tried on, ask customers to leave their own undergarments on underneath the panties. Inside the dressing room is a good place for signage about try-on policies.

A sign saying "One Person Per Dressing Room" can be posted on the door to the dressing room.

7. Shoplifting

Publicly state that you will prosecute theft. A good way to do this is on a sign behind the counter and on additional signs in any areas of the store in which it is difficult for employees to watch customers.

Have a procedure in place for what you will do if you catch a shoplifter. These policies should make it easier for you and your employees to stop thieves and to keep others from stealing as well. Often, shoplifters will tell their friends which places are easiest to shoplift from. It is best not to be on their easy-target list so that you do not get hit up multiple times.

By greeting and speaking to every customer, having clearly visible surveillance cameras, and having signs telling people they are under surveillance, you can prevent most shoplifting from occurring.

8. Accepted Payment Methods

Post a sign near the till letting customers know which payment methods you accept. For more information, see "Payment Methods," in section **3.1** of Chapter 6.

9. Employee Policies

If you have employees, have policies in place for them. As with other store and customer policies, a list of these should be provided to the employees when they are hired and also kept posted on a wall or in a binder in a staff area (so it can be easily accessed). Your employees will need to know what rules you have in place for them and what is expected of them so they can act accordingly.

Include in your employee policies how you will reward or penalize your employees based on their accomplishments and disappointments. Include codes of conduct, dress codes, drug- and alcohol-free workplace policies, sexual harassment policies, and anything else you feel is important.

When writing and sticking to these policies you can buy yourself some protection from liability. For example, if an employee is harassing another employee, the harassed employee could potentially make a claim against the employer. The employer, if he or she did not have any knowledge of the harassment, but took the appropriate action when he or she first found out about the issue, could say that the store has a documented anti-harassment policy and that it was enforced, meaning the employer had no negligence in the matter.

10. Robbery

Have an employee policy in place on what you should do if the store is robbed. Knowing what to do in this situation is very important for the safety of everyone in the store and can assist the police in capturing the perpetrator.

Often, the local police department will have classes or at least informational sheets that let you know what to do if you are robbed. Having an alarm with an alert button might speed the arrival of the police during or after a robbery.

9
HIRING EMPLOYEES

Who you hire to work at your store is an important decision that will affect how well the business runs. There are many ways you can run your store, but your answer to the following questions should guide you in deciding how to do this:

- Will the store still make a profit if you are not constantly in charge of the business, and

- Will you be able to handle the long hours and stress if you decide that you will be the main person in charge of the whole business, all the time?

If you choose to be the sole person performing all of the duties necessary to run your store profitably, you will have to spend a lot more time and energy on your business. The time and energy you spend will in turn mean that you will have less time and energy to spend on your personal life. If you value your personal time, you may have to find people to help you run the store.

Initially, finding good people to help you can be time consuming, difficult, and costly, but not spending the time or money to find good people can take even more of these resources in the long run. If you hire the wrong people, your store profits may suffer; you may find that your employees are not as competent, trustworthy, or reliable as you thought they were when you hired them.

Finding the best employees that you can to run your business can be tough, but your business will only be as profitable as the caliber of the people that perform all of the professional duties and work behind the counter.

1. Delegating Responsibilities

It can be difficult to realize how much work and time will be required to run a business if you have never run one before. Therefore, to put into perspective all of the work that will need to be performed to keep the business running, it is a good idea to write down a list of duties. After you have written this list, decide who you think would be the best person to do each duty and then place their names next to the corresponding tasks.

If you think that you will be able to do all of the work yourself, the list of duties will make it clear what you are getting yourself into. In other words, this list will hopefully make you fully realize what will be required of you so that you will be able to organize and plan your life around it. If you have decided to go into business with a partner, the list will make it clear who will need to perform which duties so that there will not be any confusion and so you will be able to divide the work evenly. The list will also help you figure out if you need to hire people to work in the store and if you would like to outsource any of the professional work (such as the accounting, website, or marketing).

Worksheet 2 is a partial list of all the duties that you will want to assign or delegate before you open your doors to the public. This list can and most likely will need to be modified to fit your own list of jobs to be performed. Using the following list as a guideline will help you start thinking about what your own list should look like. Worksheet 2 is also included on the CD so you can print it out and write names beside each duty.

This list will be well worth the time you spend scrutinizing it. It will help you to divide work evenly between all participants, allow you to figure out if you will need to hire additional people, and help you to get organized. Writing down all of the tasks that will need to be done and referencing them every once and a while will enable you to remember everything that needs to get done in the midst of being very busy. It also will not be as easy for your partner or employees to overlook a task or duty that needs to be performed when you have a list with their names next to the tasks.

2. Hiring Professionals

If you have decided that you would rather spend your time managing the store, instead of on paperwork or the website, you may consider hiring professionals for those tasks.

Before you start the business, you may want to ask yourself if you are good with your own personal finances. If you are not, what makes you think that you would be good at handling the finances for a business? Decide if you need to hire a bookkeeper or an accountant. Keeping your financial records organized is important.

If you are not the best with numbers, hiring a bookkeeper or an accountant to organize books and prepare taxes may be the best solution for you. A good accountant can advise you on how to minimize taxes payable and maximize your profits. Tax rules and regulations are complex and constantly changing, so hiring a professional could save you time and grief in the long run.

WORKSHEET 2
DUTIES AND TASKS TO BE PERFORMED

Management Tasks and Duties

1. Assign a Chief Decision Maker

    (It is important to delegate this role if you have more than one owner. You can still have multiple decision makers, but make it clear how much power over the final decisions each person has. If you have an even number of Chief Decision Makers with equal decision-making power, make a plan ahead of time that spells out how you will come to a decision if you find yourself in a deadlock.)

2. Delegate duties, responsibilities, and assignments

3. Manage employees

4. Make the employee schedule

Purchasing Duties

5. Find new suppliers and vendors (i.e., constantly bring in new merchandise to keep the store current and to make sure that you are getting the best deals)

6. Determine what new inventory needs to be ordered

7. Determine what inventory needs to be re-ordered

8. Order inventory and packaging supplies

9. Place new inventory out onto the store floor for sale

10. Change merchandise in the store window displays, on the mannequins, and on other selling tools

Marketing and Promotions Duties

11. Research and decide on the best places to advertise

12. Research the competition

13. Create advertisements and make sure any advertising purchased is cost-effective

14. Find trade shows that are worthy of attending or participating in and arrange to take part in these shows

15. Act as the company liaison and represent the company at business functions

General Duties

16. Open and close the store

17. Clean the store

18. Go to the bank (e.g., get change, deposit money)

19. Perform any new projects

20. Install any new appliances, equipment, or furniture

21. Stock office and janitorial supplies

22. Attend to computer, website, general equipment, and building maintenance

As mentioned in Chapter 7, hiring a professional web designer to create and maintain your website may be a good investment. Your website should be current and well maintained in order to keep your customers interested in your store.

3. Employee Taxes and Deductions

The employer is required to pay and collect a multitude of taxes for hiring an employee. These taxes include federal, and state or provincial taxes, and may in some cases even include local taxes.

In the US, the federal government requires employers to pay federal unemployment taxes under the Federal Unemployment Tax Act (FUTA) and also contribute to the employee's Social Security and Medicare accounts under the Federal Insurance Contributions Act (FICA). Some states also require an employer to pay state unemployment taxes. These taxes are sometimes offset by the amount an employer pays to the federal government in unemployment taxes. As an employer, you are responsible for withholding part of the employee's wages for federal income tax. The IRS will provide you with all the information and forms (e.g., W-4 and I-9 forms) to find out how much you need to withhold from your employee. The employer is responsible for delivering all of the employment taxes he or she receives to a depository that is authorized to accept federal funds. Some states also require an employer to withhold state income tax from an employee's wages.

In Canada, you are required to deduct the required taxes for your province as well as fees for the Canada Pension Plan (CPP),
Employment Insurance (EI), and Workers' Compensation Board (WCB). Contact the CRA for more information about taxes and deductions.

In order to hire employees, you must first obtain your EIN in the US and BN in Canada (EINs and BNs are discussed in more detail in Chapter 5).

4. Hiring Suitable Employees

Keep in mind that hiring the wrong employee could waste your time, cost you money (if he or she steals), or even damage your store's reputation. The old mantra of "you get what you pay for" usually rings true in terms of the quality of employees that you hire and what they are capable of doing.

The first step in hiring employees is deciding how many employees you will need to run the store efficiently.

4.1 How to find the right employees

Where to find the right people to work in your store probably depends a lot on your location and your personal network. You can always advertise in the newspaper and on Internet sites such as www.craigslist.org. The old "sign in the window" is also a decent way to get applicants. These types of advertisements have broad exposure and could get you a lot of responses. Unfortunately, many of the respondents will probably not meet your criteria.

Create a job application form to deal with people that come in who are obviously not going to cut it. That way you can hand them the form and let them fill it out so you don't have to waste your time dealing with them. If you have already opened your store, it will not take long before people start inquiring about jobs, especially if they like your store.

Hiring a regular customer may be a good way to go, especially if you have had some time to feel out his or her personality and get an idea of his or her knowledge of the types of goods you sell.

Hiring friends and family may be the easiest way — at least at first. The advantage of hiring friends or family is that you can usually trust them not to steal from you. However, hiring people you are too close to has its drawbacks. They may try to push your boundaries because they know you will cut them some slack if they show up late or leave early. Also, if things ever get bad and you have to lay someone off or fire him or her because they under perform, the repercussions can ripple through various aspects of your life. It is probably best to keep your personal and family lives largely separate from your work life, but it is true that people have been struggling, often successfully, to make family businesses work for hundreds of years and will continue to do so indefinitely.

4.2 Interviewing potential employees

What kind of people do you want working at your store? Do you want an employee that is outgoing and fun or an employee that is subdued? When interviewing potential employees, you should get a feel for their personality and how they will fit with your vision of the store and the people who represent it. When hiring for a customer service position in an adult boutique, personality is very important. Customers have to feel comfortable with the employee and the employee has to feel comfortable with the merchandise, subject matter, and customers.

Not only are you interviewing candidates for the job, they are also going to be interviewing you. They may want to know what you are willing to pay them, what type of benefits you are offering, and what hours they will be expected to work. You should be prepared to explain what the job entails and what you will give in return for their time working at your store. It may be a good idea to offer an employee discount on merchandise, which is typically around 30 percent off non-sale items.

When interviewing a potential employee, the goal should be to learn as much about the person as possible, at least as far as it is relevant to the work. The best way to do this is to try to get the person to talk, particularly about things that are relevant to the work. Ask some open-ended questions that cannot be answered with a yes or no. For example, "If a customer came in and said *(give them an example)*, what would you do?" or "Can you tell me your opinion on this product and explain why you think that?" These types of questions can get potential employees talking about your store and can show you if they can think on their feet and if they know anything about your merchandise.

When you are interviewing somebody you also need to be very careful not to ask questions that you are legally not allowed to ask. This may be even more important at an adult store than it is at other businesses because of the sexual nature of the business. You should not ask any questions that are not directly relevant to the job. The following topics are completely or almost completely off-limits in terms of legality:

- Race/ethnicity
- Age
- Gender
- National origin
- Disability
- Marital status

That may sound restrictive, but remember you can ask things that are job relevant even if they touch on some of these topics. For example, you can ask: "Do you have the legal right to work in this country and do you have documentation to prove it?" You are not asking about citizenship, national origin, or anything else that is personal, just what is relevant to legally working in the country.

It is also okay to ask, "Are you older than 18?" It is not okay to ask, "Are you older than 50?" You cannot ask, "What year did you graduate from high school?" But, "Did you graduate from high school?" is a relevant question.

You can also say, "This job requires frequent lifting of objects up to fifty pounds. Are you okay with that?" This question does not ask if the person has a disability, but if he or she can do the job. If you ask an inappropriate question, you may be vulnerable to a lawsuit.

An interview is meant to provide you with an overview of the candidate's personality. A personality shapes what a person is like, what he or she has done in the past, how he or she is most likely going to perform, and what he or she is going to accomplish in the future. The interview starts when the candidate asks for the position and ends once the person receives, or does not receive, the position.

How the candidate applies for a position at your store can be very telling of his or her professionalism right from the start. At my store, many people did not realize I was the owner and would tell me that they would love to hang out in the store and try clothes on. They would ask me what the employee discount was before they even asked me if there were any positions open. It was apparent that they wanted to work in the store for the discount and that they were not interested in actually working!

If the candidate meets your initial criteria, set up an interview. When and how the person shows up for the interview will also tell you a lot about him or her. Make sure that you have something else to do at the store that day, because sometimes the candidate might not show up, or he or she might be very late. You will not want to hire someone that is very late for the interview because he or she will most likely be late for work.

What the person wears, his or her personal hygiene, and the person's mannerisms are also very telling of his or her professionalism. If the candidate does not present an overall clean and neat appearance for an interview, he or she is not going to do so during a regular workday!

If the potential employee's mannerisms imply that he or she is not eager to impress you in the slightest and he or she is not very personable, then the person will most likely not be attentive to any suggestions or changes that he or she needs to make while working for you and it might be difficult to work with the person. Unless you are hiring the person for reasons other than customer assistance, customers will not be impressed with an unpleasant employee either!

During the interview, it is important to ask the candidate pertinent questions to to find out if he or she would be a good employee. Just as it is important to carefully listen to the candidate's answers to these questions, it is also important to watch what the candidate's body language says about him or her. If your potential employee fidgets, looks away, becomes agitated, or mumbles during a particular time in the interview, the person might not be accurately stating the true answer to your question. However, remember that the interviewee might also be very nervous if he or she really wants the position, so use your best judgment.

Some of the important aspects of a candidate's personality that you should pay particular attention to are his or her levels of the following skills and traits:

- Communication (speaking and listening)

- Self-confidence

- Responsibility

- Decision making

- Problem solving, using good judgment, and quick thinking

- Learning ability

- Reactions to other peoples' behavior

- Teamwork

- Professional attitude (such as maintaining his or her calm when he or she is upset)

Of course, it will be difficult to hire a high-quality employee without paying the person substantially more, so decide what traits an employee really needs to have to be able to work in your store and then realize that whatever additional good traits and skills you find in him or her are an added bonus! Keep in mind that even if you find the person with the best skill set and personality fit for your store, he or she might still make mistakes.

Sometimes when the interview questions are over, candidates may feel that the interview has concluded. If they say things like, "Boy, I'm glad that's over!" you may realize that they were on their best behavior during the time they thought the interview was being conducted and that they are normally not very professional.

Below is a guideline for questions to ask in an interview. Tailor these questions and create new ones that will allow you to figure out pertinent information about a candidate. Remember to check with your government agency regarding the questions you are allowed to ask.

4.3 References

Make sure the candidates provide several references and that you actually contact the references. Many people assume that all references people provide will be wonderful and do not bother calling. In reality, the people that candidates give as references tend to be honest and you can learn a lot about someone by calling.

WORKSHEET 3
QUESTIONS TO ASK IN AN INTERVIEW

Potential employee's name:_____

Potential employee's phone number:_____

Personal Information

1. Do you like working with people?

2. Do you like working with different types of people?

3. Are you comfortable talking to people about private matters, especially sexual matters?

4. Can you give me an example of a situation in which you felt uncomfortable talking to someone who was a stranger and was different from you, and how you handled this situation?

5. How open are you to new ideas?

6. Do people often ask you for advice?

7. Have you ever stopped in the middle of doing something important to help a friend with something important to him or her?

8. Do you know anything about the products carried in this store?

9. Do you have any concerns about working in an adult store?

10. Scenario Question: *Give an example of a store-related problem and then ask the person how he or she would solve it.*

Work History

11. Where have you previously worked and for how long did you work there?

12. What types of tasks and duties were you responsible for?

13. What did you like about your previous workplaces?

14. What did you dislike about your previous workplaces?

15. Can you give me an example of a difficult work situation you have had to deal with and how the issue was resolved? What did you learn from this situation?

16. Do you feel that any of your previous work experience is relevant to the work in this store? (If so, ask them to give an example.)

17. How do you think your work history has helped you become a better worker?

Education

18. Did you graduate from high school?

19. What subjects are you most interested in?

20. What subjects do you think you are good at?

21. Do you enjoy learning new skills? What do you like most about learning new things?

22. How do you continue to pursue learning?

23. Do you know how to use a computer? (You could expand on this question by asking what software the person is familiar with, especially if you need the person to work on the website, do accounting, or do other types of computer work.)

24. Do you know how to type? If so, how many words per minute can you type?

Ambitions

25. What do you see yourself doing a few years from now?

26. What would you like to get out of this job besides money?

27. Are you interested in learning more about this type of industry?

Availability

28. What days and times are you available to work?

29. Do you have a preference for the days and times you would like to work?

30. Will you work holidays?

31. What types of personal situations do you think would justify missing work?

32. If you were able to schedule your vacation time, when would you schedule it?

33. How much time would you provide your employer with if you knew you would not be coming into work for something other than illness?

34. Would you provide your employer with at least two weeks' notice if you were going to leave the position for any reason?

35. Do you have the legal right to work in this country and do you have documentation to prove it?

Scenario Situations

37. If someone came into the store and asked what you thought he or she should purchase for an anniversary gift, what would you recommend?

38. Scenario Question: *If you are hiring a salesperson, pretend to be a particular kind of customer that has a concern about a product or needs a recommendation, and have the interviewee pretend he or she is a sales employee that is assisting you.*

Simple Skill Set Test

If the employee is going to ring up sales or deal with money, it is important that they have at least basic math and literacy skills. This can be tested easily by making a very short quiz with a couple of simple math problems. For example: "If a customer buys lube for $9.27 and gives you $20, how much change do you give them back?" If you design the test well, you can test very basic literacy and math skills with just a few questions.

5. Employee Incentives

Holiday bonuses will make employees happy and are probably worth giving if employees are making big contributions and the store is doing well. Bonuses can serve to keep good employees on staff and also keep them happy and motivated. Paying out bonuses is pretty much cash out of the owner's pockets though, so it might not always be easy. The amount of bonus paid should be a reflection of how well the store is doing and the level of contribution to that success by the individual employees.

Most adult stores do not pay commission based on sales. The logistics of tracking the sales would be complicated if you have multiple employees, and the increased pressure and competition between the employees for business would most likely have a negative effect on the customers experience. Employees should be helpful and supportive of each other. Perhaps a sales target could be set for the whole store, and if employees reach it for the month or week, you would take them out for pizza or give them some other tangible reward.

6. Training Your Employees

Having well-trained employees will definitely enhance sales in your store. Well-trained people will provide better and faster customer service, which customers will appreciate.

Train your employees to be proficient with the register or point-of-sale system. Make sure they know about the inventory. This can include sizing and how to try on lingerie, corsets, and shoes. It may take some time for them to become familiar with all of the products in the adult toy section, but there are some resources available that may make this easier. California Exotic Novelties has training CDs and tests, so stores can provide training on adult toys. Their package, which they provide for free, even comes with certificates of completion! This training information covers a decent range of information about adult toys. You could also encourage your employees to read the merchandise section of this book.

7. Seasonal Workers

It may be necessary for you to hire seasonal workers for your store. The period from the beginning of October through the end of December is the busiest time of the year with many Halloween and Christmas shoppers. Valentine's Day is also big, but for a much shorter period of time — usually only the week leading up to Valentine's Day.

The problem with seasonal help is that by the time you get the employees trained, the sales season may be over. Also, some employers may hire people for seasonal work without giving them as thorough a vetting as they do their permanent employees. This is risky, because most small businesses lose more inventory and money to dishonest employees than to shoplifting and robberies.

If you have good, hard-working people you trust it might be better to try and cope your way through the busy times. Many workers are happy to put in extra effort if you pay them a little more for the crunch time or give them a bonus.

8. Keeping Good Employees

There is no one secret to keeping good employees. If you ever ask a group of employees what it would take to keep them happy, the answer will almost always be "more money!" Unfortunately, it is not that easy and most employers cannot afford to pay more for their employees, even if the employees are excellent. Pay needs to be competitive with what other companies pay people with the same responsibilities and relevant experience.

Having a pay scale with obvious tracks for advancement and raises is a good way to get driven employees interested. Other monetary rewards could include: providing earnable benefits, bonuses, and commissions. Monetary rewards do not always have to cost a lot of money either. For example, you can make employees happy if you provide them with $25 gift certificates to a restaurant or store of their choice if a customer tells you they did a good job or if they accomplished a difficult task. Acknowledging the employees' good work and accomplishments even if it is just to say "great job!" is important to most people.

Employers tend to overlook important things that will make employees happier with their jobs. These do not always cost money, but sometimes require more time from the employer in the short run. If you lose a good employee, it will take more time to find a replacement than you would have spent making sure that the employee was satisfied working for your company.

Remember to treat your employees the way you would want to be treated. Try to understand their needs and keep in mind that they are people too, and will sometimes need extra help or make mistakes. Take interest in how they are feeling, listen to them when they are talking, and be flexible with them if they are good employees. For example, give them a little time off if they are particularly stressed and you can afford to do so.

Provide your employees with guidelines so that they know what is acceptable in the business and do not have to second-guess their decisions. Provide them with opportunities to let you know how they are feeling with their job and have an open door policy in which they know they can trust you and be honest with you without incurring negative feedback or backlash. Follow through with what you say you are going to do for your employees.

If you keep the idea that your employees are important to you and your business in the forefront of your mind, and you do all the things that are reasonable and within your power to make them feel that way, it will usually keep them pleased with their work and environment. When one person is happy it is usually contagious, and everyone — including you, the other employees, and your customers — is more likely to be happy with happy people around!

Part II
Maintaining Your Business

10

Customer Service and Sales Techniques

Customer service is more challenging in an adult store because the majority of customers tend to be shy about what they are trying to find. They usually do not tell you what they want quickly or clearly. This chapter discusses sales strategies and suggestions to improve retail sales.

You may think lingerie and adult toy products sell themselves. Reality is that sometimes they do and sometimes they don't. However, you will be able to sell a lot more products if you use sales techniques and strategies. Many of the sales techniques described in this chapter are used by other retail stores, but some of the strategies are especially important in the realm of adult products.

1. Customer Service

The ability to enjoy working in customer service is something you either have or you don't have. On the one hand, not enjoying customer service can become a huge obstacle and hardship if you decide to own a retail store. On the other hand, if you like providing customer service, it makes owning a retail store a lot more enjoyable.

If you own an adult boutique in a crowded busy city such as San Francisco or Vancouver, you might have enough clientele walking through the door that you do not need most visitors to buy something. Or, you may have enough experienced customers that already know what they want (and even then, some experienced people want some assistance), so customer service may not be much of an issue for your store. But for most businesses, customer service is extremely important in increasing sales. This means you had better be prepared to listen to another person give you details about his or her sex life and be ready to answer with advice on what sort of products you have that he or she is looking for.

Much of the advice in this chapter may sound like ordinary tips regarding customer service, but it is much more important when working in an adult boutique because of the taboos about sex. Sexual repression in North America makes it much more likely that you will offend, embarrass, or provide the customer with too much or not enough customer service than in any other retail store. If the customer is not made to feel comfortable, or is made to feel perverted simply because you or your employees did not take the time to make him or her comfortable, he or she will not want to buy anything.

1.1 Greet and engage

When a customer walks in the door, allow a minute for him or her to take in the surroundings and adjust his or her body to anything in your store that might be different from where the person just came (such as the lighting or temperature). Let the customer's eyes wander a little so that he or she can take in the general feel of your store, from the size and amount of products in the store, to the colors on the walls. Giving customers time to make themselves aware of their surroundings will make them feel more comfortable with where they are, and less likely to feel pounced on by a salesperson.

After a customer has adjusted, make a sure you genuinely greet the person. All too often, it seems as though salespeople do not want to be interrupted from whatever task they are doing, or from talking to another sales associate or friend. The salesperson might look up briefly to say hello, but will then continue on with whatever he or she was doing before the customer came into the store. This gives the impression that the salesperson is too busy or that customers are too unimportant for the salesperson to give them a proper greeting. It may also make customers feel like they are playing a game of peekaboo if they have to look around the room several times to identify the person that said hello.

Don't make your customers feel like they are a distraction from the store's activities; make them feel like they are the store's reason for existing. This can be accomplished by stopping whatever task you are performing, directing your full attention to the customer, looking directly at them, and giving them a sincere smile and warm welcome.

When customers believe that the primary reason for the salesperson is to assist them, they will most likely feel more comfortable accepting the salesperson's assistance or approaching him or her with questions about products. There are several different popular approaches to welcoming a customer. One of the most popular approaches is to say hello and then ask the customer an open-ended question (so that he or she cannot say, "No, thank you."). For example, a salesperson could say, "Hello, what brought you into the store today?" Or, "Hello, how do you like our new collection of *(fill in the blank)*?" These might be good starters if you do not have a lot of time to spend with one customer; however, these types of phrases are said by so many salespeople that customers often have standard responses ready for them.

Another way to approach the customers is to treat them as if they were old friends that have just walked into your home. Greet them with a cheerful, "Good morning *(or afternoon, or evening)*" and make small talk as if you were making a new friend. Creating small conversations using such topics as the weather, the clothes they are wearing, something happening outside on the street, or conversational pieces in the store helps them to relax and enjoy their shopping experience.

By building a small but substantial rapport with your customers, you will gain enough of their confidence and trust to make them feel comfortable using your customer service. To accomplish this, you must first help them relax enough that they feel comfortable asking questions or stating concerns they have about some of the adult products. Although your customers walked into an adult boutique, you cannot assume that they are any less shy than other people when it comes to talking about mature adult content. Sometimes, in order for them to purchase the correct product, they need to describe an item or a situation; this may be extremely difficult or impossible if they do not feel comfortable speaking with you.

When customers are not made to feel welcome, the sale may never even happen. If they feel rejected because they are being ignored or they are too shy to interrupt whatever a salesperson is doing instead of paying attention to customers, they might decide to go to another store instead of shopping at your store. Almost everyone wants to feel like they are important. Providing the customers with the proper customer service attention will make them feel important.

1.2 Observe the customer's body language

You or whoever works in your store must be able to read body language and be sensitive to customers' reactions to your initial greeting. Some customers will wait for the store clerk to ask them if there is anything they might need because they are too shy or embarrassed to broach the subject themselves. Other customers might not want the clerk to ask them anything because they simply enjoy shopping without anyone's assistance, or they are too embarrassed to talk to anyone in the store. Therefore, you have to be able to judge customers' feelings by their behavior, in order to appropriately interact with each individual customer and make each of them feel comfortable in your store.

A customer's body language will tell you as much as his or her verbal language if you are paying attention to it. Many people feel shy and a little embarrassed about shopping in an adult boutique. Therefore, the timing of your words and your word choice need to be based on the customer's body language. By paying attention to this, you will know whether customers need more time in your store to feel comfortable and whether you need to speak to them in a more reserved manner before you ask them what they may need customer service help with. If you mistakenly ask customers while they are still nervous, they will not be comfortable enough to let you assist them in finding what they are looking for. They might also feel that you are being pushy if you ask too soon.

There are several body language cues that will let you know if someone is feeling a little nervous in an adult boutique. The most obvious, is when people make loud, silly, and crude jokes about your merchandise. They usually do this because they are embarrassed. Many times, a joke is an invitation for you to make them feel comfortable by laughing and then casually saying something in a serious manner, such as, "Actually, a lot of people enjoy that product." In this exchange, you are letting the customer know that it is okay to be interested in the merchandise and that other people are as well.

Customers may display other important body signals if they feel ashamed or embarrassed about being in the store, such as avoiding eye contact, crossing their arms, biting their lips, furrowing their brows, blushing, and giggling excessively. Making small talk for longer periods of time with these customers will typically make them feel more at ease. You may find them trying awkwardly to ask you questions if you make them feel like they are not the only ones interested in adult products.

Reading a customer's body language is more important for those trying to provide customer support in an adult boutique because of the additional reservations the customer might have about accepting assistance. Sometimes customers might feel awkward and afraid that they will be criticized for their interest in certain products. Thus, it is imperative to respect customers' body language and know when the they are ready to talk about the store's merchandise.

1.3 Communicate effectively

Communicating with the customers means listening carefully and providing them with the feedback they are looking for. It is not uncommon for customers in an adult store to have trouble directly describing or saying what they would like to purchase because they are either embarrassed or unsure of the products available. Therefore, the process of communicating may take longer than it would in stores that sell other types of merchandise.

It might be impossible for a salesperson to ignore all the distractions going on around him or her in order to actively listen to a customer. However, it is very important that the salesperson tries as much as possible to ignore these distractions and to not interrupt the customers. Most customers do not like having to repeat themselves, and the majority of customers in an adult store will absolutely hate to repeat themselves. Sometimes it is difficult for these customers to gather the courage to ask about a product they are interested in and having to ask the same question twice makes it all the more difficult, so they may not even try because they are too annoyed, insulted, or flustered.

More often than not, customers in an adult boutique are hoping that the salesperson can figure out what product they are talking about without having to explain what it is they are looking for in too much detail. In these instances, the salesperson has to play detective, which takes concentration and patience. It takes concentration to actively listen to a customer and patience to not assume that you know what it is the person wants before he or she finishes speaking.

Some customers need a salesperson to answer questions for clarification, especially since there are hundreds of different adult products with subtle variations. However, when the salesperson has been actively listening, he or she should be able to repeat back a customer's description and ask pertinent questions. This way he or she can distinguish specifically which product the customer is looking for. Repeating back to the customer what he or she has already said will make the customer feel like the salesperson is listening and cares about their question or concerns. Just like a good fortune-teller, a good salesperson will make a customer feel like he or she understands and has connected with them.

When customers know what product they want, it makes it easier for the salesperson to meet the customer's needs. However, more than 25 percent of the time, customers either have a poor description of what they are looking for or they do not have a description at all. Instead, they can only describe what they want the product to accomplish. Following the steps of actively listening, repeating back what they have said, and asking them questions for clarification (if needed), will help a salesperson decipher exactly what it is the customers want or need.

1.4 Discuss intimate adult issues

One of the most important abilities an adult boutique owner and the store's employees should have is the ability to discuss matters pertaining to sexual experiences in an open and mature way, while still having a sense of humor. You and your employees will need to —

- feel comfortable talking about sex with a variety of different types of customers,

- listen to customers' needs, and

- have knowledge of adult products in order to recommend those that suit your customers' needs.

If you are not comfortable talking about sex, you may want to reconsider owning an adult boutique (or at least one in which you will be providing customer service). The majority of customers shopping at adult stores are normal, fun-loving people who just want a little excitement in their daily routines and are seeking products that will help them do this. Many of these customers will ask for advice on how to choose a product. Therefore, the clerk (whether it be you or someone else) should be able to handle talking about an array of different sexual topics, from which lingerie outfit would look best, to which vibrator they should buy.

The topic of sex is still very much taboo in most parts of North America. It is often only joked about in everyday conversation or referenced on network television. In reality, sex is a major part of a normal, healthy adult relationship. Thus, many adults may find that they need to talk about their sexual well-being in order to get some advice, sympathy, praise, or simply reassurance that they are normal. These people often feel that because they are in a sex store, the salesperson will be a good confidant and adviser. Your customers will assume that you know something about sex if you work in an adult store, so get ready to hear some sordid details about other peoples' sex lives!

If you have never worked in an adult boutique or had any other job in which you had to talk openly about sexual material, try working at an adult shop to find out if it is something you would enjoy before you decide to open your own. You may find that you are not comfortable with it.

The following are typical questions I am repeatedly asked by different customers:

- "What can I buy so that I can try something new without my partner getting offended?"

- "Do goat weed or spanish fly actually work?"

- "How can I have an orgasm?"

You might not always know the right answer for every customer (especially if the person is asking you about a more serious medical or relationship problem), but most of the time, you should be able to suggest some products or at least some ways he or she can figure out the answer.

Of course, just because customers would like you to listen to a description of their sexual affairs so that you can provide them with advice does not mean that you have to listen to it — but don't expect them to buy anything then! Customers want to feel comfortable enough to buy something from you and they want to feel like they are buying the right thing for whatever they want it to do. Sometimes this involves giving them advice or coaxing them into buying something that they want but are too inhibited to try.

Listening to customers' earnest attempts to describe something personal about their sex lives in order for you to be able to recommend the right product for them should not be confused with listening to someone talk about sex in a perverted manner. You do not have to listen to someone that comes into the store for the sole purpose of getting off by telling you his or her perverted tales, and you do not have to listen to more than what you are comfortable with — even for a sale. A serious customer very rarely talks about sex in a perverted or derogatory manner, and if a person does, you may not want him or her as a customer anyway. There should always be a professional reason for listening to customers, and that is to sell them what they need, not to entertain them.

High-quality service significantly increases the likelihood of a customer buying one or multiple items. A simple way to test this is to help out ten customers who look like they don't know what they are looking for, and then to let another ten of these same type of customers fend for themselves. You will easily recognize that customer service pays off when you see how much they spend and how satisfied they are when they leave your store!

Visiting other adult boutiques and observing whether the employees help customers and get sales or do not help customers and lose sales is also a good way to test how important customer service is. Testing this in other stores is better than testing it in your own store — you don't want to lose any sales!

1.5 Recommend products to customers

The main reason that customers feel they can ask an adult boutique employee what items they should buy, is that they think the store clerk already knows everything about the products. Therefore, everybody that provides customer service in your store should familiarize themselves with all of the products sold, by learning what they are used for and how they are used. This knowledge is the key to recommending the product that will meet a customer's needs.

When employees do not bother to learn about the products and simply agree with whatever the customer says in order to make a sale, the customer may not purchase the correct item for his or her needs. For example, once a customer asked one of my store clerks if she should use a cream which had Benzocaine in it to stimulate her sensitive areas and the store clerk replied that she should. However, it would have done just the opposite by numbing the sensitive area. Fortunately, another clerk was there to recommend the actual product she wanted instead of letting the customer leave with a product that wouldn't produce the result that she was looking for. Another time a salesperson incorrectly explained to a customer how a product worked. The customer returned to the store after trying to use it and was furious because the product didn't work the way the clerk had explained.

Learning what items people like and what questions to ask them to figure out what they are looking for is equally as important as having a good understanding of the products. Therefore, you must be willing to communicate with your customers so that you can recommend the products that suit their needs. If a customer is shopping for lingerie for a partner, you will most likely need to ask the following questions:

- "What are your partner's waist and bra sizes?"
- "Does your partner have a favorite color?"
- "Does your partner like to wear long gowns, babydolls, camisoles, corsets, or teddies?"

You may need to ask these questions to understand what the customer is looking for and to give him or her an opportunity to begin a conversation with you. Starting a conversation usually makes the customer feel more at ease telling you what he or she is looking for and asking you questions about the products.

Tip: Asking customers what dress size they need is not enough information to accurately judge what will fit the person they are buying the item for! If the customer is shopping for someone else, it may not be obvious that her bust size is not relative to her dress size. Forgetting to ask about the specific bust and waist sizes can lead to the customer buying items that don't fit properly.

1.6 Create an ambiance of beauty and comfort

By creating an attractive store, a business owner sest an environment in which people feel more compelled to purchase merchandise. A lovely store coupled with salespeople that make customers feel beautiful and comfortable will inspire shoppers to buy even more items.

Almost everyone loves to feel like they look beautiful. However, getting some people to feel beautiful can be difficult. It is not hard to get women to agree that a particular lingerie outfit is pretty, but customers will only purchase the outfit if they feel like it makes them look pretty.

Often, customers who want assistance when looking for or trying on lingerie outfits (those that can be tried on) are seeking someone to tell them that they will look fantastic in the outfit they eventually choose to purchase. The role of the salesperson is to find the areas of physical beauty on the person and match it with an outfit that flatters these areas. Sometimes it is lingerie that complements customers' eyes or skin tone, fabric that flatters their figure, or a hemline or neckline that suits them. This is another reason why the salesperson should be aware of all the merchandise in the store — so that he or she can recommend items that will look the best on customers. When a salesperson has been able to make a customer feel gorgeous in an outfit, it is very difficult for the person to resist purchasing the item!

When someone needs help choosing an outfit to purchase for someone else, the salesperson may ask questions about clothing preferences and physical assets. The customer will not only want to think that the outfit is beautiful, but that the person wearing it will also appreciate it. The way to do this is to get the customer to envision the person's reaction to the present or imagine the person wearing the outfit, depending on who the gift is for.

Asking for assistance when choosing an adult toy is not easy for everyone, but harder yet is getting the customer to purchase an item he or she wants to buy but is too nervous to purchase. Customers often worry too much about what the cashier is going to think if they buy an adult toy they find embarrassing (which happens almost on a daily basis). However, there are some easy ways to make the customer feel at ease with purchasing an item. One way is to talk about the product like it is an everyday appliance.

When you have sensed, or a customer has told you that he or she feels the item would be too strange or weird to purchase, but the person still seems interested in it, let the customer know that he or she is not the first person to purchase the item. Also, let him or her know that no one working in your store will think that he or she is any different for purchasing it. A lot of the time, it just takes a moment for the customer to realize that if the product exists then it must mean he or she is not the first person to ever be interested in it!

Some of the products that customers deem strange, weird, or gross are often the most popular items. Letting the customer know what other people thought about an item and describing its features or benefits will also help to personalize the product. Once the salesperson starts talking about the item in a mature and professional way, most customers begin to relax and will end up purchasing the product. It also creates opportunities to suggest other products they might like to purchase.

1.7 Assist the customer with clothing

Starting a conversation with a customer is the beginning of building a rapport with him or her. Ultimately, this will also make a person more comfortable asking for your assistance in the dressing room later if its needed. Helping customers in the dressing room will significantly increase the likelihood of a purchase. If a customer has trouble trying on a corset or a costume, he or she will most likely not purchase it.

It can be very difficult, if not impossible, to correctly try on a corset for the first time without assistance. Some customers who were too shy to ask for help trying on corsets for the first time were either not able to put the corset on or put the corset on backwards by accident and then wondered why it didn't fit very well.

Lingerie and some costumes can be tricky to try on because of all the straps and hooks involved. Providing assistance to your customers, if needed, will ensure that the person is wearing it correctly and feels comfortable with it. It also decreases the chances that the customer will damage the item if they try it on incorrectly. If a person has a pleasurable experience trying on an item and it looks good, he or she will have a very hard time not purchasing it!

1.8 Battery-test the products

Not everyone is comfortable holding a sex toy or explaining how it works in a professional manner. This is obviously an important skill (being able to recommend and sell products to a customer), but it is also necessary for making sure that the customer continues to have a good impression of your store after leaving it, so that he or she will become a repeat customer. An important way to keep the customer happy after he or she leaves, is to make sure that you sold the person a fully functional product, especially if it is nonreturnable.

Testing adult items with batteries to make sure that they operate properly before they leave the store is a very important part of selling adult toys, and yet it may be too embarrassing for some people to do. Approximately one out of every fifty adult toys will not work properly when tested, no matter which manufacturer made it.

Testing adult toys not only shows the customer that the toy worked when it left the store, but will also show them what it does when it is turned on (if the customer does not already know). Thus, a customer cannot try and return a toy by using the excuse that the product didn't work or that it wasn't what they expected. Battery-testing toys is a good idea to gain a customer's trust and loyalty.

1.9 Be open-minded and respectful

In order to recommend products to your customers, you will have to put yourself into all sorts of different shoes. Your customers may include single, married, heterosexual, homosexual, bisexual, crossdressing, young, middle-aged, elderly, and medically-challenged people, to name just a few. This is where you need to ask yourself an important question: Are you really going to enjoy talking to different people about which sex toy might be best for their needs? If you are not willing to help customers and talk openly about the products, and instead just want to hire someone to manage the place, it might not be as easy as you think. For instance, employees may quit without notice or it might be difficult to find employees that suit your needs without paying them substantially more than you budgeted for employee pay.

Customers are usually more bold when sharing personal information about their sex lives with a clerk in an adult boutique than they would be with another stranger, because they feel that the clerk is less likely to be judgmental. Furthermore, customers might think that since they don't know the clerk, criticism will not be as hard to handle as it would be from someone they did know. These ideas and feelings are important for you and your employees to be able to recognize, respect, and be sensitive to so that you will win the customer's appreciation and trust — which will inevitably lead to more sales.

Hiring someone that cannot see any other point of view except his or her own can be damaging to your sales. For example, an employee that tells customers not to use certain products because he or she thinks they are too weird or has a personal bias against them (such as butt plugs, clit stimulators, nipple suckers, bondage items, or any type of adult movie that does not have straight couples in it). The employee's behavior may make some customers too angry or embarrassed to buy these products. Or, the customers may end up buying what an employee has recommended instead, only to try and return the product later when they realized it was not what they wanted. Hiring employees that are able to listen to the customers, recommend something they would like, explain how a product works correctly, and then let customers decide what they would like to buy for themselves are all things that are part of satisfying a customer's needs.

1.10 Deal with obnoxious customers

You will need to be prepared to deal with obnoxious customers. More often than not,

you will hear the same tiresome jokes by different customers many times over and observe adults acting very childish when they become a bit embarrassed. While some of these behaviors may be harmless, situations can become serious if customers go overboard and make rude comments about other people in the store who are within earshot of them or if they start playing with a product in a way that may damage it. Customers may also say things to you or your employees that could be considered sexual harassment.

Making sure that you, your employees, and all of your customers have a pleasant experience in your store is important, so you may need to ask some customers to keep their comments to themselves or to stop playing with the merchandise. However, sometimes you may need to ask people to leave the store if they cannot handle themselves in a mature manner.

The following are some of the annoying comments you may hear several times:

- "How could a person ever wear a G-string?"

- "Guys would never wear lingerie."

- "Does anyone actually use a whip?"

- "Will you model this for me?"

- "Only strippers wear shoes like that."

- "You have to be perverted to use one of these."

The amount of times you will hear these comments can be quite amazing! Due to hearing them over and over again, you may have to remind yourself every once in a while that your store is there so that adults can have fun. You cannot let yourself become too annoyed by these comments, because customers will notice your annoyance and not have as much fun in your store. A customer will not buy as much as he or she would if the clerk was in a good mood.

Another group of obnoxious customers are the couples who try to sneak into a dressing room together for a little bit of kinky fun. Situations like this are frustrating for store employees because their time is then spent policing the non-shoppers instead of helping paying customers. Furthermore, it creates an unfriendly shopping environment for the other customers in the store. Keeping a watchful eye on all of your customers may be difficult, but it will keep your store pleasant for every shopper and will also reduce the likelihood of theft.

If you suspect a couple has snuck into the dressing room but are not really sure, you can always ask them if there is more than one person in the dressing room. If you are uncomfortable with asking them, or you are almost certain there is a couple in the dressing room even though someone says there is not, you can always find a reason to be near the dressing rooms (such as moving merchandise around or tidying up) and listen to make sure that they are not making any inappropriate noises. Also, ask them a lot of customer service questions and listen for any changes in their tone. Most of the time, if the customers are aware that you are paying attention to them they will not do anything too risqué. Ask them to leave the store if you determine that they are indeed creating mischief in the dressing room!

It is best to keep locks on your dressing rooms so that you can control who goes into them and how many items a person takes in at once. However, you cannot completely rely on locks because you might forget to re-lock them, customers usually lock them, or a customer might go into the dressing room right as another one is leaving it, giving you no time in between. Therefore, it is best to make the dressing rooms visible from the cash register so that the clerk can keep watch on them.

2. Sales Techniques

Sales techniques are best used in retail stores only when it is to the benefit of both the buyer and the seller. When the techniques are used to also benefit the buyer, the customer will walk away with a product and experience that he or she is happy with. Repeat customers can make up a large part of your business and therefore, it is important that shoppers have a favorable opinion of your store. Additionally, happy customers make great advertisers, as they often let their friends know what their experience of shopping in your store was like.

2.1 Increase the sale amount

There are three main techniques that are highly valuable for increasing the total amount of daily sales:

- Sell the customer a more expensive item than he or she was originally going to purchase.

- Recommend other items that a customer may like.

- Suggest complimentary items in addition to the ones he or she is already going to purchase.

Explaining additional features and benefits that more costly adult toys and products may have that less expensive ones do not, or emphasizing the exquisiteness of a more pricey lingerie outfit over a cheaper one helps the customer to consider these items. In some instances, the less expensive item may be the correct choice, especially if you know that the customer has already maxed out his or her budget and you want the person to return as a satisfied customer. When a salesperson oversells, the customer will most likely not want to return to the store. Therefore, it is only appropriate to suggest a more expensive item when the customer will personally be happy and benefit from the up-sell, rather than come to regret the purchase.

A customer may not be aware of all the products that he or she would be interested in purchasing from your store. Therefore, informing the customer of similar items that he or she might want to purchase may be an easy way for you to increase the sale amount while also delighting the customer. Make sure that the additional items you highlight are either different enough for him or her to want to purchase both of them, or of equal or greater value so that you do not end up decreasing the amount of your sale.

Simply suggesting complementary items and accessories for products the customer is going to purchase can significantly increase the amount of the sale. Much like in a grocery store, customers in an adult store do not always remember all of the items they came into the store to purchase. Customers might choose an outfit or a toy that requires accessories. For example, a customer might not remember to purchase batteries or lubricant for adult toys, or may not realize that he or she needs to purchase hosiery with lingerie outfits that have garters attached to them. Making these suggestions is also a courtesy to the customer, so that he or she can immediately use the product and will not have to make another shopping trip.

2.2 Assume the sale

Giving the customer a little encouragement to purchase an item goes a long way. Customers might be unsure about making a purchase for several reasons; they may be unsure —

- Which item they like the most,
- If the person they are buying the item for will like it,
- Whether the item will do what it states,
- If the item is worth the money, or
- If they will be eternally embarrassed for buying an adult item.

Since the customer might be having difficulty deciding, the clerk can keep the sale moving and satisfy the customer's wish to purchase something by acting decisive and assuming the sale for the person.

By acting decisive, the salesperson is alleviating the customer's need to decide for themselves. If customers are afraid of making the wrong decision (especially if there is a no-refund policy in the store), then subtle suggestions from the salesperson about which product is best for them will often assuage the fear that they are not making a good purchase. Also, if they are still shy about the sale, having the clerk take control can make them feel more comfortable, as the salesperson will be taking the steps to get the item purchased for them rather than having to do it themselves.

The best way for a salesperson to act decisive when a customer has not directly asked for a decision, is to be subtle. There are physical and verbal cues that a salesperson can make to assume the sale. Some of the ways a salesperson makes a physical cue include:

- Holding the item while talking to the customer instead of placing it back on the shelf.

- Starting to fold or package the item as if he or she is getting ready for the customer to purchase it.

- Starting to steer the customer toward the cash register while holding the item.

These physical cues are often accompanied by verbal cues. Verbal cues include questions about how the customer would like to proceed with the sale, or statements in which the salesperson talks as if the decision to purchase the item has already been made or the purchase has already happened. The following is a list of phrases a salesperson can use to assume the sale.

Verbal cues to proceed with the sale:

- "Would you like me to gift wrap the item?"

- "I think this one would be much more her style, let's choose this one."

- "Shall we get pantyhose to go with it?"

- "You can't be adventurous without trying something new; this will be fun!"

- "Start with trying this one out and if you don't like it, try the other one next time."

- "You said that you always wanted to try it; now is your chance."

Verbal cues that assume the decision has been made:

- "You will need *(insert product here, such as pantyhose or batteries)* to go with this item."

- "Let me get you the accessories you need to go with it."

- "I will put this by the cashier while you look at other items."

- "Here is a bag for you to put additional items you would like to purchase in."

Verbal cues that assume the purchase has already happened:

- "This will be so much fun on your trip to *(fill in the blank)*. "

- "Her eyes will light up when she sees it."

- "Everyone at the bachelorette party will be in hysterics when they get these party favors."

- "This silk pajama will feel very comfortable and look very handsome on him."

- "This one will be much more enjoyable than your old one."

2.3 Overcome objections

When a customer is close to making a decision or has already decided to purchase an item, and then starts to waver, there is always a reason why the person has changed his or her opinion. A salesperson that has been effectively communicating with the customer during the entire selling process will usually know why the customer is changing his or her mind. However, when a salesperson is unaware of the reason, the best way to find out why is to ask the customer and not to guess. Guessing why the customer is wavering may invite other objections into the customer's decision that may not have been there originally.

Effective ways to influence the customer's decision include reiterating why he or she wanted to purchase the item in the first place, and instilling a need for urgency. A salesperson can instill urgency into a buyer's mind either by making the person believe that he or she will not be able to purchase the item again, or that he or she is going to get a good deal now but not later.

Most people know the following phrases are sales techniques. However, they are still very effective at getting the customers to purchase the items they are interested in:

- We have very little stock left and it might not be available again.

- You can't beat this sale price, so it will probably be sold out if you come back to buy it later.

- I can offer you 10 percent off the price if you purchase it today.

- The manufacturer might not make this item again.

- The quality of this item cannot be beat.

Of course, you do not want to push your customer into a sale that is not appropriate for him or her. Very often, it takes good listening and communication skills to know when and how much to pressure a customer into purchasing an item. Doing this well is very important in order to provide good customer service. You want customers to leave the store feeling like they made a good buy and wanting to shop at your store again, instead of feeling like they just got sold an item they didn't really want or couldn't afford.

To provide high quality customer service is to make sure that customers have a good time while shopping in your store, by making them feel important and informed of their choices, and by making sure they only purchases items that they feel are right for them.

11

Maintaining a Top Notch Business

Owning your own business means having to work many long hours. It can be stressful. You will need to be self-disciplined and maintain your resolve in order to get everything done right. This chapter discusses the abilities you will need to maintain a successful business. There are many skills that a business owner (especially of an adult boutique), needs to have in order to create and maintain a profitable business.

It can be easy to lose sight of why you went into business for yourself or what your goals were at the beginning, because you will not have time to reflect on this when all of your time is spent running the store. This is why some companies post the business's goals in a highly visible spot where employees can see them, and sometimes hire motivational speakers to remind employees of the company's values. These strategies are great ways to make sure employees are reminded and inspired to take action and ensure that these goals are met. You will also need to come up with some ideas of how you will remember to live up to your own expectations and goals for the business.

Listed below are ideas and suggestions to keep in mind after you have been in business for more than six months. These will warn you of some of the most common reasons why businesses fail to become or remain profitable in the long run. Figure out ways to ensure that these pitfalls do not affect you and your business and then incorporate these tactics into your daily or weekly routine.

119

1. Maintain Momentum Toward Your Goals

It can be hard to stay focused on your goals and constantly work hard at them when there is no one to tell you how your work is measuring up to meet them. If you have always been a self-motivator it may be easier for you than for other people, but everyone needs a pat on the back once in a while. Remember that your customer is your boss, especially when you are a business owner. When they tell you that you are doing a good job, take it personally. It may take a while for you to start getting compliments from your customers, but it is worth all the effort.

When reviewing your business plan, take extra time to read and analyze where you are in terms of attaining your goals for the company. You should be reviewing your business plan at least every quarter, and if your goals require a constant focus, you may want to make a worksheet to guide you.

To create a worksheet, write out your goals and see where you are along the path to accomplishing them. Then list the rest of the steps necessary to achieve goals and check off each step as you complete it.

Make sure to celebrate your accomplishment each time you reach a goal. If you write down on your worksheet what it is that you are going to reward yourself with, it can motivate you and make it fun to reach your goals! Whether your reward is having a beer with friends or going shopping, make sure that you give it to yourself so that you will have incentive to finish your next goal.

Tip: If you are very detail oriented, and you like to map out a detailed path to reach your goals, consider using planning software and Gantt charts in programs such as Microsoft Project.

2. Stay Aware of Market Trends

It is one thing to know that you have to stay aware and keep your inventory in tune with market trends, and another thing to do it. The following are ways to keep knowledgeable about the latest trends:

- Attend industry trade shows and events.

- Ask your sales representatives what is new in the industry.

- Visit stores similar to your store.

- Read current industry newsletters.

- Listen to what your customers are saying.

Make sure that you are ordering based on these latest trends and what your customers are asking for.

3. Listen to Your Customers' Wishes, Advice, or Complaints

Your customers will treat you as well as you treat them, and if you do not ensure that they are happy with their shopping experience, some other store will. Thus, if your customer has a special request for an item that you do not currently have in your store, has a complaint about something, or gives you advice on how to improve his or her shopping experience, make sure that you listen to the person and follow through on the information he or she gave you. Following through means that you would find out if you could order the item the person was seeking, see if there was a way you could amend whatever he or she complained about, and consider whether the improvements the person suggested would be worthwhile.

Your customers may not always be bold enough to tell you what they think about your store, so make sure to ask them if they are finding everything they need and if they are happy with the service they are receiving. This will make customers feel like you are concerned about their shopping experience and want to help them if they need it. By making sure that your customers are having a great shopping experience, you will show them that your store is in business to please them.

Tip: If you decide to order an item for a customer, make sure that they pre-pay for it, that you are certain the person will purchase it, or that it is a popular item that will sell in the store if the customer does not return for the item. Otherwise, you might be stuck with merchandise you do not usually carry and that could be difficult to sell.

4. Keep Prices Realistic

Be realistic and informed when you are pricing new items. Don't think that you can simply start charging more incrementally and that your customers won't notice. Do some research to find out how other stores in the area are pricing their items and research pricing on the Internet.

Listen to your customers when they volunteer information about what other stores are charging for the same item and then do some research to find out if the customers have a valid point. For example, a customer may say, "I can find this cheaper at … ." Instead of thinking to yourself, "Oh, then the customer can just go there to shop," find out if you can match that price for the customer. A better way to avoid this situation is to periodically do research, by going to nearby stores that carry the same items that you do and comparing prices. Always ask yourself, "Would I pay this much for this particular item?"

5. Continue to Advertise

Advertising is expensive, but missing good opportunities to advertise is even more expensive. As your bills begin to add up, it is easy to forget the reason that you are advertising. It is easier to add up the amount that you are spending than to figure out how many customers are coming into your store and buying your merchandise because they saw your ad.

Keep asking your customers where they heard about you because even if there is an offer in your advertisement, not everybody will remember to ask for it. When you continue to find out where your customers are hearing about your store, you will be able to ensure that you keep doing whatever it is you did to attract them in the first place.

Also, make sure you periodically create new advertisements for your store to reflect that you have new merchandise, so customers have a reason to come into the store again. When designing the advertisement, ask yourself, "Why should a customer visit my store this particular month?"

6. Avoid Financial Mistakes

Keep in mind that you are running your business to make money. There are many businesses that have gone bankrupt and you do not want yours to be one of them. The following are three main money drains to stay away from:

1. Not being able to pay back credit.

2. Organizational problems that end up costing you money.

3. Giving more money to charities than is reasonable for your store.

Starting a business credit account with wholesalers or distributors can sound like a good idea. Having credit will allow you to start selling the merchandise before you have to pay for it. The best possible scenario would be to sell your merchandise before the bill for it came, save the money you would need to pay the bill, then pay it; that way, you never have to be out of pocket for your merchandise.

However, problems can arise if a business is not able to save the money it needs or if it has not sold the amount of merchandise it needs to in toder to pay the bill. Therefore, not only can obtaining credit be difficult if you are a new business owner, but paying it back can also be a problem if you are not careful about saving the money you receive from selling items or if you purchase too many items and they do not sell. Therefore, make sure that you do not obtain credit on merchandise that you are uncertain will sell.

Organizational problems stem from not planning correctly. For example, you need to make sure that you are separating your personal and your business finances from the beginning and continue to always do so. Even if you are a sole proprietor, it is important not to get your personal and business finances mixed up, because it will become increasingly difficult to figure out which money is for what purpose. For example, you may not remember that you have sales tax due for the business and then you may spend that money on personal expenses thinking that it is extra money that you have.

The bottom line is that if you are not hiring an accountant to help you with your finances, make sure you are aware of what you need to do financially, and actually do it so you will stay profitable.

From the moment you first connect your phone line until you disconnect it and close your doors, there will be many different people and organizations asking for money or other types of donations. While giving to some charities and other organizations can be noble or be good advertising, it can also become extremely expensive. People tend to forget that most small-business owners are operating on a small profit margin. Therefore, try not to get into the gift-giving trap in which you are giving away more money than is reasonable for your business.

7. Balance Your Professional Life and Your Personal Life

Owning your own business can be very stressful on your personal life and your professional life. Working long hours — sometimes more than five days a week on difficult tasks — can lead to fatigue and make you not really want to work as hard at your business as you need to. Try to set real-istic goals so that you do not overtax your-self by trying to accomplish too much. When you set realistic expectations and you are able to meet them, keep you motivated and make you want to accomplish more.

Spending time with yourself and your loved ones is very important for leading a healthy and balanced lifestyle. It will also help you feel rejuvenated, motivated, and focused when you start working on your business again. Your family and friends will certainly be happy with you for not forget-ting to spend time with them!

If you do start to feel overworked, it can be difficult to remember why you started the business in the first place. If this does happen to you, try to remember why you began the business, refocus your efforts, hire people to do some of the work for you if you can, and begin to have fun again.

8. Remember to be Empathic with Customers

After hearing the same stories from cus-tomers over and over again, it becomes dif-ficult to remember to be sensitive to each customer's individual story. You may feel that you do not want to know about it any-more and may become impatient. However, most of these customers may not realize that their problems are shared by many other people. Since most people do not talk about their sex lives very often, they may not be aware that their problem is a com-mon one and may need someone to talk to for advice (and sometimes sympathy).

You may not want to give customers re-lationship advice, but advising them about your products, which may help them out in their situation, is part of giving good cus-tomer service. In other words, you may have to listen to their stories before they get to the point of what product they are seek-ing, and they will sometimes not want to buy anything before they tell you all about their problems. Simply try to remember that each individual is unique and that cus-tomers need to tell their own story in their own way, even if you have heard it a thou-sand different ways already.

9. Remember to be Discreet

You may not think that sex should be a taboo topic, but it certainly still is in most parts of North America (except perhaps on television and in Las Vegas). You need to keep in mind that most people want to re-main discreet about their experience in an adult store.

When you leave telephone messages for customers, run into them outside of the store, or see them come into the store with a new person, you definitely want to remain quiet about anything intimate they may have told you or anything that they may have purchased from your store until they broach the subject. You may have heard these same customers talk about topics re-lating to sex in an open, mature way, and so you may not think that they are embar-rassed about having come into your store. However, they may only have been able to talk openly because they were comfortable with you.

The fact that sex is a part of any normal, healthy relationship doesn't make it any less of a taboo, and most often people only want to talk about it in certain circumstances.

10. Keep on Top of the Little Stuff

It can be difficult to remember to do all the things you need to do in order to keep a business running in tip top shape. If you are the kind of person that likes to do everything, or you have not hired anyone else for monetary reasons, there are a lot of everyday little things that are important to the business that you may have forgotten about. Or sometimes you may say that you will get around to doing the tasks the next day and never do them because you get caught up in other tasks. For example, washing the windows, rearranging merchandise, calling customers back, or watching for new competition are all tasks that can get lost in the hustle and bustle of your workload. Some of these tasks may sound more important than others, but they are all equally important.

There are a lot of tasks that you need to remember to complete in order to convince your customers that your store is inviting, that you have the best merchandise at the best price, and that you are concerned about their experience in your store. Knowing the tasks that you have to complete in order to stay profitable and actually doing them are two different things. An easy way to remember to do all of these things and to actually get around to doing them is to create a schedule for yourself so that your tasks become just a normal part of your everyday routine.

11. Remember to Have Fun!

Remembering to have fun may sound silly, but most successful entrepreneurs are workaholics and need to be reminded of this. Having fun while operating your business will most likely lead to more sales and keep you from becoming tired of your store. Some ways to enjoy your work are to get to know your repeat customers and to try out new merchandise.

When you get to know your repeat customers, you will be better at recommending products to them. Your customers will most likely be happy that you are paying attention to what they like and that you know their names (everyone likes to hear their own name). Also, try to make your customers' shopping experience more enjoyable by doing nice things for them. For example, giving them freebies, wrapping gift purchases for them, or presenting them with in-store coupons for a later date so that they will want to come back again. If you like your customers, they will like you back and your business will become profitable.

The bottom line when owning a business is that you should work hard and play hard. If you do not work hard, your business will most likely not attain or sustain profitability. If you do not take the time to have fun, you will get tired of owning your business very quickly.

Part III

MERCHANDISE

12
Adult Toys

Adult toys are a fun, exciting, and important type of merchandise in an adult boutique. Many customers have told me that their best impressions of my store were formed by the selection, knowledge, and customer service they received when they were shopping for adult toys. Customers appreciate it when they can ask questions and get real answers. The removal of mystery and barriers from sexual enjoyment promotes sexual health, and a well-run adult toy store is one of the best ways to do this. Seeing all of the products and talking with employees that are not embarrassed to discuss adult toys, allows customers to relax and think constructively about their own sexual needs and experiences.

In this chapter I will lay out the basis for a good understanding of the different types of adult toys, how they should be used, and the materials with which they are made. Although many adult toys can be used by both men and women, I am going to divide the discussion into women's toys and men's toys, as most adult toys are packaged to appeal to a certain gender and sexual orientation. However, there are no rules as to how a person must use adult toys.

Although people are inventive and like to experiment, customers do tend to choose products packaged to suit their tastes. This is an important consideration when deciding which products to purchase for your store. Make sure that you choose the packaging that fits your clientele.

1. Materials

There are many different materials used in the manufacturing of adult toys, and it can be confusing to understand the advantages and disadvantages of each. The following section presents some basic information about the most common material classes.

1.1 Latex

Latex is a type of natural rubber that is occasionally used in adult toys. It has good firmness and softness, but it is not very durable and is fairly allergenic. People with latex sensitivities should avoid latex toys.

1.2 Glass

Hand-blown glass toys are very popular. They are sturdy, durable, hypoallergenic, and can be easily sterilized in the dishwasher, by cleaning with alcohol, or in an autoclave. People like glass toys because they are completely smooth and can be heated or refrigerated to give intense temperature sensations.

1.3 Jelly

Jelly is a term used by adult toy manufacturers to describe transparent or translucent soft plastic. Jelly can range from very soft to a rubbery firmness. This type of material is used extensively in toys of all types and may be the most common material. Jelly toys are not extremely durable and the softer the jelly the sooner it will rip, tear, or fall apart. Jelly toys wash easily with soap and water, but cannot be sterilized in alcohol or the dishwasher.

1.4 Hard plastic

Hard plastic is the cheapest material used to make adult toys. For some toys, such as the G-spot massagers, it seems to be the material of choice because a small, smooth, and hard package is desirable. Hard plastic toys typically cannot be sterilized because they almost always have electronic parts that would be destroyed in the dishwasher.

1.5 Artificial skin

All of the major toy manufacturers have their own trademarked name for their high-end soft plastic elastomer-like material, be it CyberSkin, by Topco Sales; Futurotic, by California Exotic Novelties; or UR3 (Ultra Realistic 3.0), by Doc Johnson. There is some variation as to the quality of the different brands and these may change over time, so I will base my discussion around what I believe to be the best current material: CyberSkin.

Pretty much all of the brands are made out of a blend of silicone and PVC plastic, and as a result they should only be used with water-based lubricants. CyberSkin is a very soft material that when given the right texture from molding feels astonishingly like human skin. It has just the right amount of give and pliability and is dyed to whatever flesh tone the vendor wants. CyberSkin toys are usually molded directly from various parts of porn stars' anatomies for that extra touch of realism.

Due to CyberSkin's soft nature, it needs to be treated fairly gently and washed with mild soap and water. CyberSkin toys come with a cornstarch-based powder that should be spread over them after washing to preserve the skin-like feel. If the powder is not used, the CyberSkin feels tacky to the touch and will pick up any hair or dirt it touches. The downside of using the powder is that large quantities of lubrication are often needed to fully overcome the drying and absorptive power of the powder. This is unfortunate, because the stickiness of the CyberSkin without the powder disappears with the addition of only a small amount of lubrication or saliva and it becomes quite slippery. It is probably a good idea to apply the powder before storing it, and then rinse it off before it is used.

1.6 Medical grade silicone

High-quality or medical-grade silicone is one of the best materials for adult toys. It is typically firmer than the artificial skins and some jellies, so it is mainly used in dildos, plugs, and other types of objects in which some rigidity is required. Well-made silicone toys are exceptionally smooth, hypoallergenic, and can be sterilized in the dishwasher. This makes silicone the most desirable material for high-end toys.

2. Adult Toys for Females

Many women come into my store and say, "I have never had an orgasm. Can you recommend a product to help me?"

The appropriate response is, "I can give you some suggestions, but in the end it is up to you!"

I always discuss the important things such as relaxation, comfort, mood setting, and taking time. I also recommend items for couples such as massage oils and books on foreplay.

If the reason they cannot climax is that they have partners who are unwilling or unable to do the things that would bring them to climax, or that they lack good partners, then I suggest using some adult toys. To figure out what kind of adult toys to suggest to a woman you actually need to learn a little something about her. The tricky thing about women and orgasms is that they have them most easily by receiving different kinds of stimulation. Some women can climax by clitoral stimulation alone, others require penetration or G-spot stimulation, and some require a mixture of both.

In addition to the clitoris, G-Spot, and nipples, women have a fourth less-well-known erogenous zone: the anus. Finding out what tickles the fancy of the woman buying the toy is the trick to selling her a product that she will love, as the adult toy industry definitely has just the right toy for every need and desire.

Before I describe various types of toys that stimulate the different erogenous zones, I will describe some basic vocabulary as the female anatomy is often regarded as mysterious, and there is really no reason for that. With a little bit of investigation, the various bits of the female erogenous anatomy can be understood, and with practice and experimentation, all of a woman's erogenous zones can be used to add to her pleasure and stimulation.

The clitoris is the nub of erectile tissue just above the top of the vaginal opening and just below the convergence of the labia majora (outer lips of the vagina). It is frequently covered, but sometimes protrudes from a hood of skin. In ontological terms, the clitoris is the homologous structure to the tip of the man's penis and the hood is similar to the foreskin. The clitoris is extremely sensitive and responds to very gentle stimulation. The clitoris is also the only organ a human has that seems to have no other biological role than to provide sexual pleasure.

The G-spot or Gräfenberg spot is the most mysterious of all the female anatomical features. People talk about finding it as if it moves around on women or is hidden in some remote corner of the vagina. The G-spot is no mystery and is a sort of vestigial prostate gland (I hope that does not sound too phallocentric), and is also called the urethral sponge. It consists of a region of a sort of rough, spongy tissue on the upper interior wall just on the inside of the vagina, (usually about three-quarters of an inch), and surrounds the urethral exit (pee hole). If you look, you can actually see it. Most women find a gentle stimulation of this area extremely arousing and G-spot stimulation is probably the best route to orgasm in women who normally find it difficult.

The nipples are another erogenous zone that can be used to stimulate a woman. There are a variety of toys that stimulate the nipples and most women are aroused by or enjoy gentle stimulation of their nipples.

The last erogenous zone to discuss is sometimes considered taboo, scary, or shameful to many people: the anus. For those people that have gotten over the possible objections, the anus is a very sensitive, nerve-packed, and responsive erogenous zone. Obviously due to bacterial considerations, some attention needs to be paid to basic hygiene and contamination control, but with a little attention to detail and some soap and water, this really becomes a nonissue.

When starting to think about anal play, think small, slow, and well lubricated. Many people try anal play and say, "I didn't like it. It hurt!" As I said earlier, the anus is very sensitive and it is easy to make oneself or someone else uncomfortable. If it hurts, the person was probably trying an object that was too big too fast, or without sufficient lubrication.

Many women are capable of climaxing regularly through anal stimulation alone and some claim that the rectum has "clitoral legs" that run from the clitoris to down around the rectum. At the very least, the G-spot is often stimulated through anal penetration, as the vaginal wall (the tissue separating the vagina from the rectum), is very thin and elastic and the angle of the rectum tends to direct pressure towards the G-spot.

2.1 Dildos

Probably the oldest sex toy in the world is the dildo. These have been found sculpted out of wood and ivory dating back to ancient times. A dildo is a solid phallus shaped object.

The best of these are made of medical grade silicone (which gives toys a good firmness and stiffness that is not too hard and not too soft), are made by companies such as Tantus, and come in all shapes and sizes.

Blown-glass dildos are also very popular and, like the silicone, have some hygiene advantages over other materials as they can be sterilized. Unfortunately, both the glass and silicone materials are significantly more expensive than the other materials (except for maybe CyberSkin, which would typically carry with it the branding costs of the material and of the porn star that it is modeled after).

Glass dildos range anywhere from clear glass in very simple shapes, to intricately colored and designed glass with all sorts of knobs, ridges, and spirals. The elaborate ones can sell for hundreds of dollars, although functionally equivalent ones can be very reasonably priced. Glow Industry's Don Wand line is an example of excellent function and value, and Phallix Glass is an example of elaborate sophistication.

Glass has high thermal mass, so if a glass toy is put in the refrigerator or microwave it can stay cool or warm for a while. Some women enjoy the stimulation, while other women find the glass too hard. The vagina is a soft place, and toys made of silicone, which has some give, can make things more comfortable for sensitive women.

2.2 Vibrators, G-spot stimulators, and rabbits

There must be at least 10,000 different models of vibrators currently on the market. They are sold in every shape, color, and complexity with styles that look like everything from penises, to fruit, to insects, to ex-presidents! When a customer is trying to decide on a vibrator there are many aspects to consider. Material and feel, vibration strength and adjustability, durability, cost, water resistance, size, and shape are all important aspects that affect the performance and enjoyment of a vibrator.

The strength of the vibration is important as some women like extremely fast and strong vibrations and others prefer slower more oscillating vibrations. The ability to adjust the intensity of the vibration is a valuable feature, as the woman can tune the intensity to fit her mood.

The outer material of the vibrator determines how it feels and its softness. Almost all vibrators have a hard plastic inner part that contains the electronic mechanism and are coated with another material, usually soft plastic, artificial skin, or jelly. The outer material is molded into a variety of shapes that are too numerous to discuss in any detail.

Shapes that have a hook near the end or a bulge at or near the top are probably intended as G-spot stimulators. G-spot stimulators are toys designed to focus the stimulation on the G-spot. They are often much narrower in the shaft than conventional vibrators, are bent near the end, and often have a bulge or an egg on the tip. The good ones have the vibration mechanism in the bulge on the end, and the angle allows a woman to gently pull the toy against the top wall of the vagina to give the G-spot direct stimulation. Many of these toys resemble a small egg on the end of a short crooked stick.

Rabbits are a newer type of vibrator and were brought to international attention when they were prominently featured in an episode of *Sex and the City*. Rabbits have several parts that work together. The main vibrator part is usually shaped much like a penis, with a hard plastic base where the control unit is built in. The rest of the device is usually made out of translucent, soft jelly-like plastic.

Inside the shaft is a conventional vibrator, and a series of beads hooked to rotating mechanisms of various sophistications (which serve to make the beads rotate around the shaft, often changing directions rhythmically). This makes the Rabbit have a series of moving, massaging nubs in the middle of the shaft. The tip usually has a mechanism that makes it wiggle around in a circle.

The Rabbit name comes from a little jelly rabbit that sticks up from the bottom of the shaft (the rabbit faces the shaft and its ears point towards the tip of the toy). The body of the rabbit is a vibrating egg type mechanism and the ears are long and jelly. When the shaft is inserted, the rabbit can be positioned so that the ears touch either side of the clitoris and give it a good stimulating. All of the mechanisms can be controlled independently to make this a very dynamic and involving toy.

Rabbits are hugely popular and definitely a top-five best-seller in the toy category. These toys are so popular that the industry has had to move well beyond Rabbits in search of ways to expand these lines, and now you can find similarly constructed toys called dolphins, hummingbirds, flowers, and much more.

2.3 Clitoral stimulators

For many women the route to an orgasm is direct stimulation of the clitoris. Clitoral stimulation products are very popular and many women seem to like them because they feel good, but also because they tend to be smaller, cuter, and less imposing than a large phallus-shaped object.

Probably the single best-selling adult item in my store is a very small waterproof vibrator called the Mini Might. It was designed as a clitoral stimulator rather than a vibrator for insertion. It is a powerful little vibrator with different attachments for the flat end that make it either smooth or nubby. Another bonus to this toy is that it is waterproof, so a woman can take it into the bathtub. Remember that for a woman to climax, mood can be very important, so the

ability to take a little toy into the bubble bath with a glass of wine might be just the ticket!

Another important class of clitoral stimulator is the butterfly type. These often resemble a butterfly in design and have straps that go around the legs and waist that hold the vibrating mechanism tightly against the body. A wire-connected remote control is used to control the intensity of the vibrations. These products may seem a little cumbersome, but they do sell and have been around a long time.

Adding a little suction to vibrating clitoral stimulators can add another layer of pleasure. There are a number of clitoris-suction devices on the market, some of which work well and some of which are essentially fakes. The ones that work well have a jelly cup that goes over the clitoris and then either a squeeze ball or an electric suction pump to add the vacuum. A vibrating bullet or mechanism is usually located nearby. There are a few devices marketed as clit suckers that have a suction cup on the end, but no way of adding the suction. These products really do nothing.

2.4 Vibrating remote control panties

What will technology provide us with next? These panties have a pocket in the front, into which a vibrating mechanism is inserted. This mechanism can be controlled from as far away as across a large room via the remote control. Customers have told me stories about a husband holding the remote in his pocket while at a party where his wife was wearing the panties. He could make her start grinning and giggling with the touch of a button and nobody was the wiser. This product was fairly popular but was not cheap, so it was more of a luxury item.

A much cheaper version of this technology is a remote control vibrating bullet or egg. The bullet is intended to be inserted and a little soft wire antenna dangles out. The control works the same way and this costs less than half of the panty version.

Rumors have been going around in the industry that in the near future, versions of remote control panties will be introduced where the vibration will be controlled via cell phone, giving unlimited range!

2.5 Nipple stimulators

Nipple stimulators range from clips to vibrating suction cups. These are a moderately popular class of items. The less-expensive nipple suction devices, which are very good at suction but have no real frills, sell more than any of the more expensive and elaborate vibrating types.

Classic nipple clips with little dangles or a chain connecting the two clips are inexpensive and also fairly popular.

2.6 Electric tongue

The electric tongue is a jelly tongue that has a mechanism that makes the tip move in a circular licking motion, with adjustable speeds. This is a popular item among female customers.

2.7 Fukuoko or fingertip massager

The Fukuoko brand of fingertip massagers was the first version of this I remember seeing, and others followed suit after it's huge

success. The original Fukuoko is a fabric glove that has small but powerful vibrators built into every fingertip. These are powered and controlled by a battery pack mounted near the wrist. The glove is not an overtly sexual toy, and feels incredible when it is rubbed down the back. The intensity of the vibrations makes the person's skin tingle.

Fukuoko also sells individual finger tip plastic pieces with no glove. These make for a very intense clitoral stimulator and can also be used for point massaging.

2.8 Dual penetrators

Dual penetrators are variations on either the dildo or the vibrator, and are designed to provide both vaginal and anal stimulation simultaneously. Although there is no doubt that many customers would benefit from this type of stimulation, these might not be the ideal tools to accomplish it. The sales, at least in my store where I carried a couple variations, were occasional, but never very common.

2.9 Strap-ons

Strap-ons are dildos or vibrators that are strapped onto a woman (or a man pretending to have a different penis) where a penis would be.

These come in a variety of styles, many of which involve little thin straps connected to a dildo or vibrator. You should assume that products that have thin straps do not work or easily break. The best strap-ons use harnesses that are often sold separately or in sets with detachable toys. These harnesses have nylon webbing straps and often a felt pad and a metal or rubber ring on the front, in which a wide variety of toys can be mounted. These are comfortable and the toys are solidly positioned so they can be used hands-free.

SportSheets manufactures a well-designed harness that is sold with silicone dildos by Tantus. These give you the advantage of interchangeable attachments and sturdy, long-lasting construction.

If you are stocking your store and aiming for a lower price point, you will end up with some cheap strap-ons. Do yourself a favor and order a few of the high-quality harnesses as well. If you have customers asking about them, you can always sing the virtues of the more expensive harness, and be honest about the shortcomings of the others. You might be surprised at how many customers would be willing to go up in price to get the better product.

2.10 Anal toys

First off, anal toys are equally applicable to both genders. I will discuss this in more detail in the male toy section, but men can be stimulated anally much the same way as women. The most popular anal toys are the small plug-like toys such as the Silicone T or the Tantus Bend Over Beginner silicone toy. Both of these toys are made of high-quality hygienic silicone and are small enough to be comfortable for beginners in anal play. The small anal toys are great when used simultaneously with vaginal or oral sex. The traditional plug-shaped toys are still popular and are now available in silicone and in many sizes.

2.11 Ben Wa balls

The Kegel muscles are the muscles that line the pelvic floor in men and women. One way to exercise your Kegel muscles, is to stop and start peeing by contracting and relaxing the muscles. In a woman, these are also the muscles involved in orgasm contractions and childbirth. Doing Kegel exercises is believed to give more intense orgasms as well as ease childbirth and recovery.

Ben Wa balls are small, heavy, metal balls that are placed inside the vagina. When a woman walks around, she has to contract the muscles of her vagina to keep the balls from falling out, giving her Kegel muscles a good work out.

Candida Royalle's product line Femme sells a variety of ergonomic-looking vibrators and toys including a Kegel exerciser. This exerciser is a very thin object with one end shaped roughly like the inside of a woman's vagina. This is used in much the same way as the balls; however, it is a little heavier, anatomically designed, and much more efficient at giving the specific exercise.

3. Adult Toys for Males

Unlike some women, most men are not searching to find out how to have an orgasm. They already know how to orgasm. Men are more likely to be searching for something that is a little different, or that just feels really good. Men's toys come in a variety of types and typically involve stimulation of the penis or the anus. Most of the anal toys, in terms of functionality, are the same for men and women, so the only type I will discuss in detail are the prostate stimulators. As for penis stimulation, pretty much all of the toys are classified as one of several types of masturbators. Even though the focus of my shop was geared much more to couples and women, I still did brisk business in moderately priced men's toys.

3.1 Prostate stimulators

Many people do not know, but men have a hidden erogenous zone: the prostate gland. This is a very similar structure to the female G-spot and it is very sensitive. The prostate can be massaged by sticking a finger or object into the rectum and rubbing or pushing gently against the ventral wall (towards the testes). The prostate is very sensitive and some men might find the experience a little too intense and uncomfortable at first, but this is usually because it is so rarely stimulated in this way. With gentle stimulation, this can lead a man to climax, and many claim that if they have sex or masturbate while their prostate is being stimulated that the orgasms they have are much more intense.

Prostate stimulators are an interesting class of products. Aneros sells a prostate stimulator product that comes in many sizes and variations. It consists of a probe-like projection with a lump on one side that when inserted pushes against the prostate gland, and a handle-like piece that has a bent extension on one end that pushes against the skin in between the testes and anus. As the man moves or thrusts during sex, the handle-like part is pushed on by his body, causing the probe-like part to rhythmically massage the prostate. This enables a strong and hands-free prostate massage while the man is having sex. This product is definitely not recommended for men that have premature ejaculation problems.

3.2 Masturbators

It has often been said that all a man needs to get off is somewhere tight and wet, and that is exactly what masturbator toys provide. Despite the simplicity of the concept, there are some basic differences that make some of these toys much better than others. The material they are made out of is the most important factor in quality. The artificial skin or CyberSkin toys are by far the best, but masturbators also come in jelly-like, soft plastic, and latex. The jelly toys are the next best material, and the soft plastic and latex toys are at the bottom of the pile.

The stretchiness of the softer CyberSkin and jelly materials is really a big performance advantage. The size of the toys is a major factor in price and can also affect how they are used. Some are designed to be smaller and handheld, while others are intended to be set down and used hands-free.

As previously mentioned, most of these CyberSkin toys are molded directly from porn stars' private parts and branded with their names. These personalized effects are really just cosmetic, and more attention should be paid to the size, shape, and angles of the holes, which are what affect the depth and the position at which they can be used.

From a purchasing and placement standpoint, I would recommend stocking a variety of the smaller and cheaper versions of the CyberSkin and jelly products, as they will sell well. You should also carry a few of the larger and more expensive ones, in effect creating a tiered pricing structure, in which you have a variety of good products available at different price points. By stocking as few as ten types of these toys, you can get most of your customers placed with the appropriate product that is the best they are willing to pay for.

Many of the masturbator products come with vibration tools. These tend not to work very well with the toys and should not be a major determining factor for anybody purchasing them.

3.2a Virtual sex toys

Recently a product has come out that links a CyberSkin masturbator toy to a home computer via a USB cord. This allows a man to use the toy as a controller of sorts and interact with various pornographic video game scenarios. At the time of this publishing, the technology is very new, but shows a lot of potential and is likely to turn into a web-based activity with all sorts of different applications. I would recommend researching this on the Internet or seeking it out at an adult toy convention to find out the latest developments.

3.3 Sex dolls

The classic blow-up doll has been around a long time and used in many comedy movies and music videos. The classic plastic blow-up doll is still available and can be purchased inexpensively. The cheaper dolls are much more suited for novelty roles and gag gifts than sexual satisfaction.

A process of incremental advances has created a range of higher-functioning sex dolls that range from the $50 versions of the old-fashioned dolls with added Cyber-Skin vaginas, to the $5,000 RealDoll which weighs as much as a real person and is custom-made for every customer. The ultra high end RealDolls are only sold by that company directly to the customer.

People frequently buy the cheapest dolls as gag gifts and occasionally buy the moderately more sophisticated inflatables with a few higher end features. I do not stock any dolls with retail prices of more than $100,

as I don't think the frequency of sales at a higher price point would justify the use of space in my store.

Hustler sells a life-size solid latex doll for between $400 and $500 and I see many shops that carry it, but I honestly do not know how well they sell. I'm not sure that there are a lot of men who would buy a sex doll for that kind of money, especially if it requires having a store clerk help them lug it out to their cars.

3.4 Pumps

Pumps are made to suction the man's penis to enlarge it. Many customers purchase these in hopes that they will increase the size of their penis indefinitely. The pump will suction the penis to increase its volume. However, when the pump is taken off and the suction disappears, so will the increase in volume. Sometimes men purchase them as play toys as well, but less frequently than when they are hoping to increase the size of their penis.

3.5 Prosthetics

Prosthetics are a popular item despite many people cracking jokes about them. They actually do increase the size of the penis through rubber or other material attachments.

3.6 Cock rings and lassos

A cock ring is a metal, rubber, or silicone ring that is worn around the penis and testes. The ring is supposed to fit tightly and the squeeze it gives prevents premature ejaculation and can help to maintain an erection. The cock ring has evolved from just a simple ring to a female pleasure-adder, as many of them also have all sorts of knobs, bumps, vibrators, and projections that are designed to stimulate the clitoris and anus during sex.

A lasso is similar to the cock ring in concept, except instead of a ring it is a loop of rubber tubing with a bead on it that can easily be tightened around the penis and testes by sliding the bead down towards the loop of tubing.

4. Bondage Toys

Bondage is the use of restraints in sexual play. An entire sub-industry exists called BDSM (the short way of saying Bondage, Discipline, Domination, Submission, Sadism, and Masochism). When people in the adult industry think about bondage, they think about leather, vinyl, latex, ropes, masks, ball-gags, and medical instruments. I believe it would be hard for a person who was not personally involved in the BDSM community and scene to do well with a store that carried a lot of these products, and it would be hard to integrate much of the equipment and paraphernalia into a typical strip mall.

The high quality, handmade leather and vinyl masks, clothes, and straps used by serious BDSM practitioners are very expensive and often custom made. Specialty stores and online retailers typically cover this market, and although there is plenty of room for more businesses, it may be difficult to have a successful BDSM store in your area.

An adult boutique should provide the basic supplies that beginners or people that are not real BDSM types would be interested in. These include silk ropes, door cuffs, handcuffs, SportSheets, whips, crops,

and paddles, which are discussed in the following sections.

4.1 Silk ropes

A little tie up is always fun and something most couples experiment with. Since bondage rope is almost always applied to bare skin, it is really nice to have a rope that is sturdy and yet soft and non-abrasive. Japanese-style silk ropes seem to be the optimal solution, and virtually all major adult wholesalers carry some of these in a few colors and lengths.

4.2 Door cuffs

There are many types of cuffs that strap around or under the mattress or onto bedposts, chairs, and other pieces of furniture. However, door cuffs are one of the most popular of these variations because a person can use them in any room with a door.

Door cuffs are usually made of fabric and Velcro straps that can be attached to the wrists or ankles; these straps are attached to a hook that is thrown over a door. This leaves the person who is strapped in partially immobilized and stretched up the door.

Customers will not usually request door cuffs, because they are an item that does not typically come to mind. However, when the customers see door cuffs for sale and they are interested in a restraint system, they will often purchase them.

4.3 Handcuffs

People associate handcuffs with authority and power. They work really well in dominant/ submissive role-play and allow couples to say to each other, "You have been naughty; I need to lock you up."

Despite the psychology of the handcuffs, they are still hard and uncomfortable to wear. My store carried some very basic inexpensive metal handcuffs, but also some slightly more expensive fur-lined handcuffs. Both sold well, but for couples who are not into pain and want to play with handcuffs, I strongly recommend the fur-lined ones. They provide the same functionality (as they are the same as plain handcuffs), but with much more comfort.

4.4 SportSheets

SportSheets are a great invention. The main sheet is a fitted bed sheet that feels much like a sturdy cotton sheet, but is reinforced with a few nylon-webbing straps that run under the mattress and prevent the sheet from slipping. Four Velcro pads, which are about five-inch squares, can then be stuck to the mattress anywhere on the fitted sheet. On each pad is a little metal clasp that connects via a short chain to a sturdy Velcro cuff that can be used on the wrists or ankles. The Velcro pads cannot be pulled off the sheet by pulling on the cuffs, but are easily disconnected by grabbing them at a corner and peeling them off.

The SportSheets eliminate the need for a four-poster bed for tie up fun and allow for an unlimited number of positioning options. Plus, they are a form of safe and sane bondage in which a person can be completely immobilized and yank and tug away all he or she wants without going anywhere. If the person wants to be freed, he or she can grab the corner of the pad and peel it off without too much trouble.

4.5 Whips, crops, and paddles

Whips, crops, and paddles come in many fun forms. These types of slightly naughty, but still comfortable implements are very popular. The expensive ones are very nice, but in my store customers are sensitive to price when it comes to the purchase of these toys.

You can buy a cat-o'-nine-tails whip made of rabbit pelts or with velvet tails. Suede whips also come in pretty colors such as pink and make for good, but not too painful fun. One of the newer types of whips is made out of the same type of rubber material as a Koosh Ball and is available in sizes from key-chain small to a pretty thick bunch of rubber pieces about two feet long. This makes for a fun and unintimidating toy. I recommend carrying a small variety of each in a few colors.

Riding crops sold in adult stores are usually about two feet long and have small tags at the end of a one-inch paddle. Like almost all the other adult toys, there are exceptions to this rule. Some of the most popular riding crops are the ones that most resemble a real riding crop, and those that have about a two-inch by two-inch paddle on the end. One of the paddles has a shiny, red leather heart at the end and the other has a paddle is that shaped like a hand.

Paddles can come in many colors, lengths, and widths, such as leopard print, fake fur, and black leather. Paddles with shapes and words cut into them (like hearts or the word "love") are especially popular. When someone is hit with one of these, the image or word written on the paddle (usually in mirror image), is left as a red mark on the skin.

13
CLOTHING AND SHOES

An adult boutique can differentiate itself with style and customer service, but actually selling merchandise is the store's purpose and the source of all revenue. This chapter is designed to give you a basic understanding of the different types of clothing typically carried at adult boutiques. Good knowledge and understanding of most of the jargon, pitfalls, choice brands, and things to look out for will be a big help when it comes to ordering your inventory.

1. Lingerie

Lingerie is the secret weapon of the modern adult boutique; it serves as valuable merchandise as well as decoration. By stocking your store with lots of well-displayed, colorful, and beautiful lingerie you can really make your shop look great. Pretty and colorful displays can really set a romantic mood, and an extensive selection will bring

in a wide array of customers, many of whom would not have felt comfortable walking into a bookstore-style adult store.

As a general rule of thumb with lingerie, it pays to keep abreast of the latest fashion trends of the season you are buying for, as the styles are always changing. Be sure to stock a wide range of sizes from petite to plus-size, as they all seem to sell well. Also, stock a lot of colorful lingerie. People have strong likes and dislikes for colors, and you shouldn't limit yourself to red, black, and white. On several occasions couples have come into my store and said things like, "Wow! Green silky lingerie! We have to buy it because we love green."

Lingerie is usually sold in a set, such as a bra and a pair of panties. This makes items easier to merchandise and a little more cost-effective than individual top and bottom pieces. These sets sell well, but a recurring problem is that women who are a size four on the bottom can also have D-cup breasts (thanks to nature or the wonders of modern medical science). Since many matched sets will not fit an individual woman's proportions, it is wise to also stock a variety of separately-sold tops and bottoms. You will want to watch out for customers mixing and matching sizes within sets. The easiest way to do this is to have the cashier check the sizes of separated pieces at the point of sale.

1.1 Bras

The following list describes common lingerie products and features:

1.1a Underwire

The term "underwire" refers to the reinforcing wire under the bra cup. It serves to give the bra a defined shape and evenness. It is good for adding symmetry and structure to the appearance of breasts.

1.1b Padded and push-up bras

The most common type of bra worn today is the padded underwire bra. This bra has a rigid underwire and padding of varied thickness and placement. The padding makes breasts look bigger and also serves to hide the nipple outline that can sometimes be seen through a woman's clothes.

Some padded bras have foam padding covering the whole cup and others have most or all of the padding on the bottom of the cup. More padding at the bottom serves not only to make the whole breast look larger under clothes, but also pushes the breasts up and together. The result is more cleavage, which can be dramatic. Despite the amazing potential of these push-up bras,

many are not lingerie in the traditional sense, and clients will often be looking for something more bedroom oriented.

1.1c Shelf bras

Shelf bras are constructed like the typical padded underwire bra, in which the breast is supported from below and lifted by the padding, but there is no fabric covering the front and the nipples are exposed.

1.1d Open front

Often open-front bras are very stringy and lacy, but sometimes they are built sturdier with underwire. Any built-in sturdiness is not really important though, as this bra is designed entirely for its look, and isn't mean to provide support. The breasts hang naturally and are fully exposed.

An attractive variant of this type of bra has sheer pieces of fabric that come up and over the breast, but the fabric does not connect in the middle and the nipple is left exposed.

1.1e Strapless bras and dress tape

Strapless bras are specialty bras that are designed to be worn under strapless dresses or dresses that would not look good with visible bra straps. These come in a few different styles, but one particularly popular design uses adhesive pads that attach to the skin on the sides of the breasts, sort of under the arm.

These, along with dress tape (which is used to adhere extremely low-cut dresses to the skin to prevent fallout), are popular items that people will come looking for in more sophisticated lingerie and adult shops, as they still seem a little on the fringe for many mainstream retailers. Customers are frequently looking for these items to wear with evening gowns, wedding dresses, and prom dresses.

1.1f Non-underwire bras

Non-underwire bras range from fairly normal to extremely delicate and barely there. Some women prefer a bra that has no underwire, padding, or solid structure. These bras show off the natural shape of a woman's body and are very common in the lower-cost lingerie sets. More geared for a sexy dance than a day at work, the simple and often sheer elegance of these bras is perfect for a little romance.

Another advantage of the non-structured design is ease of fit. Sets sold in small, medium, large, and extra-large are often this style as you do not have to worry about a specific cup size; however, larger breasts may not be as well covered or may bulge a little, and smaller breasts may cause the fabric to drape a little. Still, it is great for your store when you are able to fit a popular item to almost everybody with only four sizes, and these types of tops and bras help make that possible.

1.2 Panties

Everyone knows what panties are, so this will be kept brief. The basic definitions of the current popular panty styles are provided.

1.2a Thong

The fabric on the back of thong panties is very narrow. When worn, part of this fabric disappears between the bum cheeks.

1.2b G-string

G-string panties have a cloth patch in the front, but the rest of the panty (the waistband and the back) is just a string or ribbon.

1.2c Boy shorts

Boy shorts are similar to a really small pair of shorts. They ride very low on the hips and are cut very high at the leg holes, often letting the bottom-third of the wearer's bum cheeks hang out the bottom. These are available in a wide variety of styles, including ruffled boy shorts, which are popular for wearing under short dresses, miniskirts, and costumes.

1.2d Open-crotch panties

The name open-crotch panties says it all. These panties have a loop that each leg goes through, but they are not connected in the middle. There are many styles to choose from, the lacy butterfly being a popular classic, and no adult boutique should be without a selection of at least a few styles of crotchless panties.

1.2e Novelty undies

Panties in the novelty category include those made out of candy or those with funny animals attached to them (which are typically attached to the penis area of male underwear). Candy underwear, including bras and other edible clothing, are just as often purchased by people intending to wear them for their partner as they are as gag gifts. The funny looking animal underwear is typically only sold as a gag gift.

1.3 Babydolls

Traditionally babydolls are sleeveless and loose-fitting short dresses, or waist-long dresses, and are made out of silk or cotton. Modern styles of the babydoll now include those that have fabric attached to a bra-like part. In many styles the fabric wraps around the back and is open in the front, making a loose flowing style that shows off the belly and panties. Babydolls are still commonly made out of silk or cotton fabric; however, lacy and sheer babydolls are also popular.

1.4 Teddies

These lingerie outfits resemble one-piece bathing suits, except that they are made out of lingerie materials such as lace, cotton, or mesh. Often they are crotchless or have snaps at the crotch. The classic black teddy seems like it will never go out of style. A teddy in the fashionable color of the season can also make for a good seller.

1.5 Hosiery, garter belts, and body suits

One of the anchors of any good lingerie store is an adequate hosiery section. Customers shopping for hosiery usually seem to know exactly what color and style they want and are disappointed if you do not have it. It is very important to expend some effort building the display and inventory for this section.

For example, a person may come into your store looking for red fishnets, but these come in several cuts and also different types of netting. Because there are so many choices, you should personally help the customer to find what he or she is looking for. Show him or her the different styles of red fishnets. He or she might say, "Oh, I wanted them in the type of netting with the big holes and without the toes." This can be a little frustrating if you don't carry that specific style, but those are the breaks of selling something with so many variables.

My recommendation is to cover your bases. Have the normal black fishnets in pantyhose and stockings in all sizes and in small, medium, and large nettings. Since it is difficult to carry all the hundreds of different types of pantyhose and thigh highs, carrying less of the extreme colors, sizes, and designs is a good option. In my store we carried most of the product lines from Shirley of Hollywood and Leg Avenue with a few styles filled in by other vendors.

Do not let people try on stockings or hosiery products. It is not hygienic, they are easily damaged, and they are almost impossible to return to their original packaging once they are removed. It is a good idea to keep a few samples so that people can feel the different fabrics and see the product out of its package. This may help customers decide whether or not they would like to purchase an item.

1.5a Pantyhose

Pantyhose are stockings that go all the way up and have a waist. A small selection of standard pantyhose is useful for people who want to buy a pair to go with the rest of their purchase, but most people would rather buy them elsewhere, as traditional pantyhose is usually much cheaper at other types of stores. Therefore, carry mostly fishnets and other interesting styles.

Fishnet pantyhose tend to be crotchless, as there would be little coverage in this area anyways, due to the netting. There are currently many different types of printed pantyhose that have various patterns and seaming on them. Many of these are trendy, and can give a sexy and interesting look that can't be accomplished by run-of-the-mill pantyhose.

Also, many women like the French or Cuban Heel styles of hosiery or stockings, as these are harder to find in other stores. In this type of pantyhose, the bottoms of the feet and the heels of the stocking are reinforced, and therefore opaque. This reinforced section comes up the back of the heel and ends in a point, which then becomes a seam that continues up the back of the leg. The seam is often in a color that contrasts with the rest the the stocking, so the line is a decorative and sexy detail.

1.5b Stockings

Stockings are like long socks and are usually described as knee high or thigh high. The thigh-high stockings are the most popular for pairing with lingerie and usually require a garter belt to stay up (unless they specifically state on the packaging that they have extra elastic around the top to keep them from falling down). All of the fabric styles available in hosiery are usually available in stockings as well.

One of the main aspects that determines how high-end a stocking is, is how elaborate the top of it is. Stockings will almost always have a little bit of lace around the leg hole, as this helps reinforce them, makes them tighter around the thigh, and provides a place for the clips from the garter belt to attach. Fancier stockings have more lace, sturdier lace, more intricate lace, or other decoration along the top.

1.5c Garter belts

Garter belts are just what they sound like: a belt-like piece of lingerie with little straps called garters that hang down and attach to stockings. I would say that it is probably better to carry simple garter belts. The basic black, red, and white colors will fill most of the customer's basic needs. This is especially true now that many of the lingerie sets (including skirts, shorts, corsets, and bustiers) have removable garter straps as part of their design. This means that many outfits can be worn with stockings without a garter belt, and therefore less variety is needed.

1.5d Body stockings

Body stockings are like pantyhose bodysuits. They can be sleeveless, but many have long sleeves that end by looping around the thumb. These are available in many of the same fabric styles as hosiery and stockings, and almost all are crotchless. The crotchless feature is not solely for the sake of being risqué, but also for practical reasons, as getting in and out of them is a delicate operation and a trip to the bathroom would be very difficult if you had to take the whole thing off.

2. Pasties and Breast Petals

Pasties and breast petals work similarly, but fulfill very different purposes.

2.1 Pasties

Pasties are small decorations that are adhered to the nipples and hide the nipple and most of the areola. They are often little cone shaped glittery cups, sometimes with tassels or flat stickers. There are also more elaborate versions, that may be made of feathers or plastic flowers. Pasties are sometimes used in topless bars in states where archaic liquor laws prevent the exposure of the nipple in the presence of alcohol. They are also very common in burlesque, and have become a sort of mainstay in adult entertainment and role-play. Usually the pasties come with glue, but it is a good idea to stock a few bottles as well.

2.2 Breast petals

Breast petals are flower-shaped pieces of sturdy cloth with glue on the petals. These are glued tightly to nipples, which appear to vanish under them. Their purpose is to allow thin and delicate fabrics to be worn without the nipple showing through.

3. Corsets and Bustiers

Corset is a term that is frequently used incorrectly to describe a bustier, but these are actually two different types of clothing.

3.1 Corsets

A corset is like a cinch that goes around the waist and does not cover any part of the breasts. It is supposed to fit very tightly and give a sucked-in stomach and hourglass shape. It is typically laced up in the back, but nowadays most also have a zipper in the front. In the past, a woman had to be tied into a corset by someone else. Now, a woman can put a custom-tied corset on and take it off by herself using the front zipper. Corsets are actually not all that common nowadays and seem to be largely confined to a more

Gothic or bondage and sadomasochism (BDSM) crowd, which is frequently looking for corsets made of vinyl or leather materials.

3.2 Bustiers

The bustier is having a real rebirth and is becoming more widely available in many styles. A traditional bustier is very similar to a corset, except that it continues further up the woman's torso, and typically stops just above the nipple. This allows the garment to not only cinch the waist, but also push up the bottom half of the breasts. This produces ample cleavage and is probably what you think of when you picture the romance novel pirate's wench, with the big skirt and the heaving bosom.

Bustiers are still readily available in the traditional sturdy and rigid styles, with heavy duty lacing on the back and steel or hard plastic boning to protect their shape.

They are also common in more decorative styles. These maintain the fit and appearance of the classic bustier, but are made of more delicate and lightweight materials. They cannot be used to squeeze the breath out of you like the old ones, but they look pretty and often have lots of ribbons, bows, and sheer bits. This new type of bustier often has detachable garters (for the people who want to wear them with their jeans) and comes with panties. Bustier tops are so popular that some slinky evening dress styles include them as part of the dresses.

4. Club Wear and Minidresses

The line between what people wear in the bedroom and what people wear out of the house is becoming blurrier all the time. Lingerie manufacturers have responded with a vast array of very sexy and seductive outfits that aren't traditional lingerie, but are also a long way from normal everyday clothes. Minidresses with ultra short skirt-like bottoms and fabric that is so thin and tight it leaves very little to the imagination, and pants and tops with open sides, are all becoming more common and popular. Exotic dancers may have been the first target demographic for these styles, but interest in them seems to be contagious, as they are also becoming very popular with the general public.

The increasing popularity of parties and club nights where sexy clothing is a must, such as the Exotic Erotic Ball, are encouraging many people to push their personal limitations and experiment with what they would wear in public. Customers are aware that adult-oriented lingerie stores are really the only retail outlet for these types of clothes.

5. Sexy Costumes

Sexy Halloween costumes are all the rage. The month of October was always the best month of the year at my store. In fact, the week before Halloween was always an absolute madhouse of young women hunting for the perfect ultra-sexy costume. The big lingerie vendors such as Leg Avenue, Shirley of Hollywood, Dreamgirl International, and Coquette International Inc., have really gone whole hog into the costume business. Orders for costumes need to be placed well in advance, as the popular ones always seem to sell out, and it is important that you stock a variety of sizes. I would place my biggest costume orders in April for delivery at the end of August.

As for what types of costumes to buy, think cute and sexy and you won't go wrong. Like with lingerie, it is important to order the costumes that are trendy. Also, pay attention to price point, as some that look really pretty run a little steep and many customers are turned off by very expensive costumes since they are only likely to wear them once or a few times. Costume sales also provide a fantastic opportunity for up-selling or add-on selling. "Okay, now that you have picked out your costume, have you found a pair of shoes and a wig to go with it?" is a common sales pitch that works.

In my store, a particular sexy, black cop outfit outsold the next best-selling costume at least two to one a couple of years in a row. I stocked that costume and a few others (such as sexy maid and nurse outfits) year-round. People love to role-play and the classic nurse, cop, and maid outfits seem to be favorites. They sell fairly well all year long, and particularly rapidly in October.

Stocking a lot of costumes for Halloween that you can sell throughout the whole year will benefit your store for two reasons: First of all, you do not want to run out of costumes during the Halloween season, so by having more costumes you will probably not run out. Second of all, if you end up having a large oversupply of costumes, you will be able to sell them throughout the year without having to put them on clearance.

6. Swimsuits

Swimsuits are not an easy product to stock. Depending on where you are located, sales are often highly seasonal, there may be a lot of competition, and good ones tend to be pricey, meaning that you cannot get as big a markup as you can with other types of lingerie. If a lingerie retailer wants to try to make some swimsuit sales, especially in response to a spring buying season, my advice is to stick to a few classic and sexy styles, in a number of colors, and at a reasonable price point.

If your shop caters to or is in a high-end and high-price market, you might be wise to stock the sexiest, smallest, and highest fashion suits you can find. There is an abundance of very sexy, very beautiful swimsuits, many of which seem to come out of Brazil.

If you do business that isn't as price inelastic, then you will need to stick with more moderately priced vendors. Stock suits that are sexy enough that people will be able to justify buying them at an adult boutique, but not so skimpy that they will be afraid to wear them. These types of suits seem to sell best and fill the niche.

Designs that fit this class often have very low-rise bottoms and/or are very high cut from below. The tops are smallish or have designs such as hearts or butterflies cut out of some of the fabric. One-piece suits can also be very sexy if the fabric has gaps or cutouts over parts that would normally be covered, even if they do not reveal anything X-rated. It can also be a good idea to stock a few colors of lower-cost, barely-there, string and thong bikinis, as there is a market for them and there is a relatively small amount of space and cost associated with doing so.

7. Shoes

Shoes are frequently an underappreciated lingerie accessory. My store predominantly carried shoes made by Pleaser USA Inc. They have several lines and sell everything from sandals to some serious fetish-style, nine-inch heel, leather ballerina shoes. My store sold a great deal of cute and inexpensive shoes from them and did consistent business selling high-heeled pump and shiny platform styles. High-heeled and platform boots also sell well in the winter months, especially during the Halloween season, as a costume accessory.

Price your shoes competitively, as customers can be very price conscious. The Pleaser brand I carried allowed the store to have very reasonable prices on shoes that look elegant and sexy.

When my store first opened, I carried a black pump-style shoe that had a nine-inch heel and a four-inch platform. They were pretty wild looking, but when anyone tried them on they looked like they were going to fall or roll their ankle. This made me really afraid of liability, so I called the vendor to see if I could return them. The vendor told me that they, and most other exotic shoe companies, indemnify the stores from customer injury lawsuits and that they were not keen on taking them all back. I marked them down in price to try and get rid of them quickly and then did not order any more. To me it was not worth the risk of selling something that seemed dangerous or had the potential to cause a customer to suffer an injury in my store. This is just something to keep in mind when looking through shoe catalogs.

14

Accessories, Novelty Items, and Adult Movies

Depending on the type of store you decide to open, there are many different accessories and novelty items that you can sell. If you have the space to sell them, accessories and novelty items can add a great number of additional sales and increase the average amount of a customer's purchase.

If you decide to carry movies, the selection will depend on the type of store you have. For example, if you have a store that you are trying to keep less hard core, you are probably not going to want to sell movies that have people performing sexual acts on the cover or genres like S&M.

1. Accessories

Accessories may include such things as wigs and jewelry. Small accessories, such as jewelry, can be kept close to the till or on the counter beside the till to encourage customers to buy them at the last minute.

1.1 Wigs

My store sold a lot of high-quality wigs. There was steady business, with customers shopping for wigs throughout the year and most often near Halloween. My store carried Henry Margu Wigs exclusively. They make synthetic wigs that feel very much like real hair. Because the material is synthetic, it can be dyed almost any color, so there is a wide selection of wigs in colors ranging from white to neon to natural hair tones. Some of the wigs even glow under black light.

You can buy wigs in unnatural colors such as pink and purple, and wigs in various tones of blonde and black. However, natural colors such as browns and shades of red did not sell well in my store. The most commonly sold wig lengths were bob-cut and about two inches longer than shoulder-length. These were not cheap costume wigs and had the fit and finish of high-end salon wigs, even though the prices were pretty reasonable. Most wigs in my store sold for $50 or $60, depending on the length of the wig and how stylized it was.

Henry Margu Wigs will last a long time if cared for properly. Specialty wire brushes need to be used, or the hair can be pulled from the netting. A wig conditioner can also be used occasionally to prevent frizzies. If you are going to sell wigs, it is a good idea to sell wig accessories as well. Customers may also appreciate it if you sell foam heads for a few dollars, so that they will have an easy way to store their wigs without crushing them.

In my store, I originally had the wigs displayed in such a way that it was easy for customers to try them on. I soon found that many people thought trying on wigs was really fun and a good way to kill some time. This got to be a bit of a problem so I raised (and expanded) the wig shelf and put a up sign that said, "If you are interested in purchasing a wig, please ask for assistance." I still let customers try on the wigs, but the game was not as much fun when they had to ask the clerk for each one. This also prevented the wigs from being damaged by people horsing around.

1.2 Body jewelry

Many adult boutiques carry body jewelry for piercings, such as belly button and tongue rings. This market is becoming increasingly crowded, but the markup can still be pretty good if you are able to find a good vendor.

It is important that you buy high-quality body jewelry for piercings, which are usually made out of medical-grade stainless steel or titanium. Body jewelry is also sold in PTFE or acrylic materials, which have the advantage of being dyeable, glow-in-the-dark, or UV fluorescent. The PTFE (also known as Teflon®) material is nonallergenic and can be sterilized, and is a better choice than acrylic materials (which are not nonallergenic or able to be sterilized). Conventional body jewelry is sold in gauges, which range from 000-gauge (which has a shaft diameter of 10 mm) to 18-gauge (which has a shaft diameter of 1.02 mm).

Vibrating tongue rings are the ultimate hybrid of adult toys and body jewelry. The Tiggler is a small and powerful vibrator mounted on a stainless steel post that acts as a tongue stud. If a person does not have a tongue piercing and wants to try this out, the vibrator is also sold with a little rubber band that a person can use to fasten the device to his or her tongue.

In addition to the body piercing jewelry, my store did well selling waist chains and toe rings. A waist chain is like a necklace that is worn around your waist, and is especially sexy with a bare midriff outfit. Fine jewelry and fancy costume jewelry also sold well, by itself and as an accessory to outfits being purchased. Necklace and earring sets were popular, as were tiaras. The tiara business has a brisk existence during the spring wedding season.

2. Novelty Items

Bachelorette parties are very popular, and what is a bachelorette party without a bridal veil tiara with little plastic penises stuck to it? My store sold a lot of these cheap party favors and gags. The following novelties seemed to be the most popular items.

2.1 Gift bags

Gift bags are very popular with men and women for a variety of occasions. My store carried shiny gift bags with photo pictures on them of everything from hunky men and scantily clad women, to giant erect penises. People bought gift bags as gags for everything from bachelorette parties and birthdays, to retirement parties.

2.2 Games

Party games and more intimate games designed for couples spending romantic time together were both popular. Party games for bachelor and bachelorette parties included Pin the Macho on the Man or Pin the Boobs on the Babe, trivia-type games, and dirty cards. These games tended to be reasonably priced and were good sellers. Drinking games were also good sellers, but did not seem to be as popular.

The games meant for couples can either be reasonably priced or much more expensive. Those that sold well in my store included Strip Poker, dirty dice, coupon books, and foreplay games that were economically priced. The higher-end games usually didn't

sell as fast because they are most often sold as add-ons to other purchases and weren't the primary reason the customer came to shop.

2.3 Books and Magazines

Customers are choosy when it comes to buying books. Some of the most popular books include how-to books relating to the subjects of Kama Sutra, tantric sex, massage, and female orgasms. There are also novelty books such as *101 Nights of Grrreat Sex*.

Some stores also sell adult magazines. Women- and couple-friendly adult stores often do not sell magazines because they tend to be more hard core and have graphic nudity on their covers. The adult stores that do sell them vary in the selection of magazines they carry. There are a lot of different magazines genres, including women and men of specific ages, specific anatomical features, and specific sexual orientations. Some of the popular titles of adult magazines include: *Hustler*, *Barely Legal*, *Penthouse*, *Penthouse Letters*, *Playgirl*, *High Society*, and *Swank*.

2.4 Decorations

Decorations are primarily geared towards bachelorette and birthday parties. Men tend not to decorate for bachelor parties as much as women do, but they do purchase decorations as well.

Beads, banners, confetti, straws, cookie cutters, ice cube trays, balloons, and many other little trinkets are very popular in the bachelorette crowd. Big sellers are naughty cake pans and Lollicocks. Candies are sometimes great sellers, but they are often made for the novelty and not so much for the taste. Therefore, customers appreciate it when you can recommend items that satisfy both of these requirements.

2.5 Gift cards

Dirty greeting cards are a must. These range from just random jokes to occasion-specific cards, and customers seem to buy them for a wide range of special occasions. If you negotiate with your vendor, they will often throw in a display rack with your first decent-sized order of greeting cards. See the Resource Guide on the CD for a list of Adult Greeting Card vendors.

3. Adult Movies

Adult movies really are the glue that holds the whole adult industry together. Virtually any sexual activity you could possibly imagine can be found featured in an adult film. For this reason I will not attempt a comprehensive review of adult movie genres. Instead, I will discuss the best way to purchase and stock adult movies, and also highlight adult DVDs that should be carried by even the most classy and elegant adult boutique.

3.1 Movies for couples

Not all adult movies are created equal. Many feature hard-core, male-oriented sex from start to finish; however, there are a handful of studios that break that mold.

The former adult star Candida Royalle started a studio called Femme Productions, Inc., in the 1980s. The films made by Femme Productions are some of the first female-written and -directed adult movies. These films are genuine adult movies featuring real sex between men and women, but they also feature romance, relationships, kissing, and emotions. Men will probably find them a little slow, but most women will find them entertaining, nonthreatening, and erotic.

Another studio, Adam & Eve, has made many movies that also feature plots of varying sophistication and depth. Some of them are made well enough to be fun to watch even without the sex. They represent a decent middle ground between the highly female-oriented movies of Femme Productions, and the hard-core movies with no plots from most modern studios.

The Adam & Eve and Femme Production movies are a fantastic opportunity for couples that are interested in watching an adult movie together, but are nervous or turned off by all of the hard-core titles on the market. A good example of this kind of movie is *Pirates*, which was a joint venture between Digital Playground and Adam & Eve, and features many big-name stars, on-location shoots, special effects, and a budget of more than a million dollars. This high-budget feature has a plot that closely parallels the *Pirates of the Caribbean* story, and it really defines a new level of production value for adult movies. *Pirates* demonstrates the drift into mainstream media that the adult movie industry is currently enjoying.

3.2 Sexual instruction DVDs

Sexual instruction DVDs are popular and bridge the gap between mainstream and adult movies. Some videos that cover topics such as intimacy and massage are really in a gray area, and others are much more clearly lying on the adult side of the line.

Ex-porn star Nina Hartley has her own line of instructional DVDs all titled *Nina*

Hartley's Guide to … . They cover everything from sensual massage and adult toys, to anal play. These movies are fairly informative and show direct demonstrations by Hartley herself or by attractive male and female models.

The Alexander Institute also produces a line of detailed sex education DVDs in its *Loving Sex* series. Even though these DVDs feature real sex, they have a much more clinical feel to them than the Hartley DVDs and, as a result, might not be as much fun for a couple to watch. The Alexander Institute's DVDs do tend to contain information that is a little more detailed and that can be very useful for expanding a person's sexual knowledge. This can be especially helpful if the person is in a position where expertise is an advantage (for example, if you are a customer service employee at an adult boutique).

Instructional DVDs sell moderately well and add a touch of credibility to an adult movie section.

3.3 Ordering adult movies

You usually end up paying more or less the full wholesale price if you order the most recent adult movie releases or specific titles you are interested in from studios like Femme Productions. This can make the retail sale of these movies fairly expensive. Shortly after the *Pirates* movie came out, my store was selling it for roughly $60. That particular movie was so popular that it still sold well at that price, and the women-oriented movies, which were a little cheaper, also did fairly well. In general, however, it is the budget-priced adult movies that really fly off the shelves.

Once you have established a good relationship with a movie wholesaler you can buy adult movies at unbelievably good prices. I typically buy boxes of 50 movies. Each box is filled by the vendor with a variety of titles all along the same general theme or made by the same studio. These vary in price (typically from $1.50 to $5.00 per DVD) based on the demand and status of the content. This allows me to have a fantastic markup and still offer inexpensive movies, and makes it easy to do deals such as "buy two DVDs and get one free" promotions that really encourage sales.

When you buy bulk boxes of movies, you typically have control of the genres and studios, but not the titles. If there is a particular movie you want to carry or a customer requests a certain title, you need to order that title specifically and, to do that, you will usually pay several times the bulk price. If you have a good relationship with your vendor, they may be able to see what they can do to get a specific title into the box, but that can be difficult (and do not expect it to happen if it is a new release).

15

Bath and Body: Lotions, Lubricants, and Condoms

A large variety of products fall into the bath and body category, including items with different uses, qualities, and packaging. Whether a store only carries basic lubricants and condoms, or carries everything from body dust to lambskin condoms, almost all adult stores sell some products in this category.

1. Body Lotions, Creams, and Gels

Kama Sutra, as well as a number of other manufacturers, sell a variety of wonderful smelling and tasting products for use in an intimate setting. These have several purposes, and range from massage lotions and flavored dusts, to shaving creams. The list is constantly evolving and growing, and which product is best is really a matter of personal preference. I will highlight a few choice items and cover some of their advantages and disadvantages. These are important to understand, as customers constantly need help differentiating between these products and almost always want to know their advantages and disadvantages.

In my store we put open bottles on a little table and let people use Q-tips to sample the smells, tastes, and feels of the various products. Customers really appreciate the ability to try the different flavors and often get excited when they find something they really like.

1.1 Body dust

The first body dust I learned about was called Honey Dust and was made by Kama Sutra. There is now a variety of nearly identical products on the market that I believe are mostly follow-on competitors. My store carried only the Kama Sutra line and it was very popular despite the fact that it is not cheap.

Honey dust is a very fine glucose powder (a type of sugar). It has been infused with various scents and flavors and is dusted onto the body with a feather duster that is included with the honey dust. A light coating of this dust can help prevent wetness and gives a very nice, very mild scent to the person. Once applied, it can last several hours on the body and a partner will get a pleasant and tasty surprise if they lick or kiss the wearer of the dust. Basically it makes a person taste like a mildly sweetened and flavored piece of candy. The effect really is worth the money!

1.2 Massage lotions

There are several types of massage lotions available. Some give a pleasant warming sensation when rubbed into the skin, an effect that is created by the ingrediant Methylparaben. Massage oils come in at least three categories, which are explained in the following sections.

1.2a True massage lotion

True massage lotion is serious, get-down-to-business massage oil. Nothing enhances a massage like a truly wonderful massage lotion, but this type of oil is rarely edible and cannot be used as a sexual lubricant.

A good massage lotion is made of a thin but persisting oil. There are a wide variety of oils available in a multitude of scents; some have warming properties and some do not. It seems that all of the top-grade massage lotions use oils that are not edible. That is not to say that they are toxic, but you would not want to consume very much of them. Because these are truly oil-based, they are not recommended for use during sexual intercourse. They are also definitely not latex compatible.

1.2b Warming massage lotions that can be used as lubricants

Recently, several makers have marketed warming massage lotions that can be used as lubricants. K-Y®Brand is a recent but very high-profile entry into this market. The catch is that some of these types of products are typically second-rate lubricants and third-rate massage lotions.

In my opinion, once you have used a true top-grade massage lotion and a top-grade lubricant, it is hard to make the compromise. Then again, these products are geared to a more entry-level clientele, not the experienced connoisseur. These products can be an easy first step for a couple that is interested in trying new products and expanding their intimate and sexual experiences (figuring out what level of product the customer is ready to try out is actually an important role of the sales staff at an adult boutique). A little fooling around with some warming oil is a great place to start for a couple looking for ways to make things interesting.

1.2c Edible warming oil

Edible warming oil is a massage lotion that cannot be used as a lubricant. I have not yet seen an edible, warming, sexual-lubricant massage lotion, but I would expect that the best sexual-lubricant massage lotion researchers in the world are actively pursuing this!

The edible warming oil, such as the Kama Sutra "Oil of Love" line, is an interesting compromise. It is a great product to use during foreplay, as it allows a person to give a decent massage with a very nice warming effect on the skin. Afterwards, the person can lick the oil off of his or her partner as much as he or she wants, anywhere! Although some people may use this as a lubricant, I would not recommend it as one.

1.2d Glow-in-the-dark massage lotion

Glow-in-the-dark massage lotion is very popular, but is difficult to find in non-adult boutiques. This type of lotion is a fun alternative to the usual massage lotions and also comes in a variety of tantalizing scents.

1.2e Body cream

Body cream is a popular type of thick cream that couples use, either to massage with or simply to have fun smearing on one another. It comes in a variety of scents, and depending on the ingredients, can also make for edible fun. The product is popular with couples and with those looking to purchase a gift. A popular brand of body cream is Body Butter; note that this is different from the body butter found in drug stores that is meant to nourish the skin.

1.3 Desensitizing gels

Desensitizing gels use benzocaine to numb the skin. This is generally marketed from two angles by differently-branded products.

The first type are oral desensitizers, such as Kama Sutra's Original Pleasure Balm, Good Head, and a spray called Deep Throat. The oral desensitizers can be used to slightly reduce the gag reflex and make deeper oral sex less uncomfortable. The Pleasure Balm by Kama Sutra is a popular one. They have expanded the Pleasure Balm line to include flavored variants that contain no benzocaine and are not desensitizing, but instead are slightly tingly due to the menthol in them, which gives a sort of cool and warm feel at the same time.

The second type of desensitizing gel is geared at fighting premature ejaculation and prolonging intercourse by desensitizing the man's penis. All of these formulas are pretty potent and tend to numb everything they touch; therefore, if a man applies the lotion to himself, whatever he touches will become numb as well (unless he washes it off).

1.4 China Shrink Cream

China Shrink Cream is a cream that has been marketed for a long time and claims to tighten up the vagina. I have not heard any explanation that would lead me to believe that this product actually works, but customers request it on a very regular basis.

2. Body Paints

Body paints come in a variety of different colors and ingredients (such as water- or latex-based). Another popular type of body paint is glow-in-the-dark.

Water-based or edible paints are most often sold in kits that include brushes for applying the paint. Latex-based paints are usually sold in individual plastic tubes or small glass bottles that resemble nail polish bottles, and do not typically come with any accessories unless the person purchases a starter kit. You can purchase accessories separately (like foam rollers or foam brushes) to apply latex paints. These items are often purchased by couples or as gifts. The cheaper versions of the product are usually purchased as gag gifts.

Edible body paints can either taste awful or be rather tasty, which is often reflected in the price.

Tip: Make sure that any chocolate body paints that you claim are edible really are edible! Some chocolate body paints refer to the color of the paint rather than actually being made out of chocolate!

3. Herbal Supplements, Enhancers, and Pheromones

There are a lot of adult products on the market that make a great number of claims. Some are fairly new and some have been around for ages. Real Spanish fly is actually a cantharide compound derived from a beetle that is toxic, but can result in erections that will not go away. It is illegal in North America and used only for animal husbandry. You can order Spanish fly supplements from any major adult wholesaler and you can be fairly certain that it will be safe, cantharide free, and completely ineffective.

Horny Goat Weed has an active ingredient called icariin and is derived from a plant of the Berberidaceae family. There are Chinese research studies that show in vitro that

icariin has effects that can mimic Viagra in some aspects, but it is a lot less potent. The actual effects of taking a Horny Goat Weed supplement is not yet clear.

There are many sexual enhancers on the market, such as Vigel for women (with L-Arginine), erection arousal creams, and penis enlarging creams. While these items also sell well, you cannot always be certain that they will do what they state on their packaging.

You may also run into human pheromone products; however, these are basically just perfumes, as no human pheromone has ever been identified.

4. Sexual Lubricants

Lubricant is the product that people understand the least and have the most questions about. The truly excellent lubes are a little pricey, but are good sellers with customers who already appreciate them and with those who can feel the difference between them and cheaper brands; therefore, you should always have store testers available that allow customers to feel the difference in quality. I will recommend some specific brands, but a lot can be known about a lube just by reading its ingredients.

4.1 Oil-based lubricants

The traditional oil-based lubricants are almost all gone from the market thanks to the rise of the silicone-based lube. Condoms still carry warnings about not using them with oil-based lubes, even though these lubes are now only marketed as hard-core male masturbation products. A boutique-style store can easily get by without selling these products, as there are plenty of alternatives, such as Happy Penis Cream, which is designed for male masturbation and is sold in cute packaging that sells well in adult boutiques.

4.2 Silicone-based lubricants

The original high-strength silicone lube is called Eros. There are actually two companies marketing similar products with this same name. After a prolonged legal battle over who was the original, it seems that they both will be allowed to continue selling their products using the Eros name. I have felt both and like the product from Pjur the best. After seeing the incredible popularity of Eros, everybody that was able to has thrown their hat into the ring and begun making high-strength silicone lubricants. ID Millennium, ID Velvet, and Wet Platinum are also very good brands.

The ingredients in these lubes are all variations of synthetic silicone, such as dimethicone, dimethiconol, and cyclomethicone. These synthetic silicone ingredients are hypoallergenic, colorless, and tasteless, and are the main active ingredient in many good hand lotions. These lubes do not feel like hand lotion though — they are unbelievably slippery, never dry out, and never get sticky.

If you have never tried a high-quality silicone lube, it is worth checking out. A little drop is all you need (and you will not need to reapply). One warning though: if you spill any you need to clean it up with soap and water, as it will not dry up and will remain slippery indefinitely. These lubricants are condom safe, but manufacturers recommend they not be used with silicone toys.

4.3 Water-based lubricants

K-Y Jelly is probably the worst quality lube on the market today. It disappears almost as fast as you can apply it and it gets really sticky as it starts to dry. It also tastes terrible. Astroglide and Pjur Basic are two top-quality water-based lubes and, to be fair, K-Y Liquid is a huge improvement over K-Y Jelly. These lubes are still not long lasting, but are very slippery and much less prone to stickiness than their older Jelly cousin.

The main ingredients in water-based lubes are propylene glycol and glycerin. These ingredients are also hypoallergenic and nontoxic. Even the best water-based lubes are not as slippery and do not last as long as the silicone lubricants.

4.4 All-natural lubricants

All-natural lubricants are not as common, but are starting to become more popular. One of the best made lubricants of this kind is made by Secrets Down Under, a company based in Australia. They tend to be more expensive, but are very good for the skin, as they have ingredients in them such as sweet almond, coconut oil (an exception to the oil lubricants mentioned above), and vitamin E. The lubricant can also be used as a nice massage oil because of these ingredients. Since these are washable ingredients they will not stain the sheets, and therefore are a good alternative to silicon-based lubes if customers are afraid of stains. However, using condoms together with an oil-based lubricant is not safe.

4.5 Flavored lubricants

Flavored lubes have been around for a while, but have had a bit of a renaissance in the last few years. They used to taste horrible, but have improved and become top-quality water-based lubes that taste like real candy. The ID Juicy Lubes and Wet Flavored series are two great brands of flavored lubes. I have known couples where one partner was never comfortable giving the other oral sex, until they discovered that a good smothering of watermelon flavored Juicy Lube was all it took to solve the problem.

I highly recommend stocking the small pillow packets that you buy in mixed-flavor tubs in addition to the bottles of flavored lube. When my store started carrying these lubes, I would throw a couple of pillow packets into customers' bags as a sample and gift. People really liked them, and I believe that it effectively created an awareness of the available product lines.

5. Shaving Lotion

Body care is important to many customers buying skimpy lingerie. As a result, adult toy makers have started marketing lines of hair trimmers and groomers, and the makers of lotions and potions have started to offer products such as shaving cream. My store carried a very good shaving cream called Coochy Cream. The first customer that came in asking for it was actually a balding man that used it to shave his head, as it left him smooth and moisturized.

Coochy Cream is available in a few different scents and is very popular. It has a sort of cult following, in which people walk in and are excited when they see that my store carries it. This is always a little surprising to me, as I have never seen any advertising for the product, and yet people seem to know all about it.

6. Condoms

Besides lubrication, condoms are the only other product that is sold in all adult stores. Condoms are sold singularly or in packs, and come in a variety of sizes, shapes, colors, and materials. There are also many different brand names; some brands that sell well are Trojan, Durex, Vivid, and Tastee's. The following list is of the main types of condoms.

6.1 Latex condoms

Latex is the traditional material that condoms are made of. They come with various features, lubes, shapes, sizes, and textures. Since grocery stores, gas stations, and drug stores carry the usual varieties, I would recommend that an adult boutique specialize in the more interesting variations. The Vivid brand, created by a high-end adult movie studio, has a line of high-quality condoms that sell very well in an adult boutique. In addition to the Vivid line, you should focus on those that are flavored, colored, oversized, or pleasure enhanced with bumps and ridges.

6.2 Polyurethane condoms

Durex sells a condom called Avanti that is made of polyurethane. They claim that it is thinner than a latex condom, but I have felt it and don't think that it feels any thinner than the good latex condoms that make ultrasensitive claims. However, the polyurethane is less susceptible to chemical breakdown than latex, and is good for people with latex allergies.

6.3 Lambskin condoms

Lambskin condoms are among the most expensive varieties. Customers that like them tend to be allergic to latex, or are more pleased with the way that lambskin condoms feel. These are made from lamb intestines, and their large pores are believed to make it easier for sexually transmitted diseases to pass through them; however, the pores are still small enough to prevent sperm from passing through. Due to their high price tag, these condoms are not fast sellers.

6.4 Female condoms

Female condoms are not a big seller, if they even sell at all. Studies of female condoms have found that they are hard to insert and remove, and that they have a higher failure rate for preventing pregnancy than regular condoms. If you are curious about them, you could order some and check them out, but do not expect your customers to buy them.

Other titles of interest from Self-Counsel Press!

Ask for these titles at your local bookstore
or visit our website at www.self-counsel.com

START & RUN A BED & BREAKFAST

Monica Taylor and Richard Taylor
ISBN: 978-1-55180-803-1
$21.95 USD / $22.95 CDN

Includes a bonus CD-ROM to help your
business planning!

- Develop a plan for your unique
  B & B
- Be your own boss
- Learn from successful B & B
  operators

Have you ever stayed in a bed and breakfast
and thought about how exciting it would
be to open your own B & B? It takes more
than dreams and a spare bedroom to
achieve success. With a keen business
sense and the advice in this helpful, easy-
to-read guide, you too can turn your home
into a welcome place for visitors to stay.

FINANCE & GROW YOUR NEW BUSINESS

Angie Mohr, CA, CMA
ISBN: 978-1-55180-820-8
$18.95 USD / $19.95 CDN

Get a grip on the money!

- Raise capital for your small business
- Measure risk and plan for
  profitability
- Grow your small business profitably

Entrepreneurs need to know how to measure the effectiveness of their operations,
human resources, and marketing in order
to pinpoint inefficiencies and maximize
profits. This book outlines all the ways to
raise capital and then make it work for you!

CD CONTENTS

The following information is included on the enclosed CD-ROM, in PDF format (for use on a Windows-based PC).

- Resource Guide
- Questions for Wholesalers Worksheet
- Tasks and Duties Worksheet
- Interview Questions Worksheet